FIFTEEN to FIFTY

MEMORIES OF AN ORDINARY BOY

Don Moggs

Pen Press Publishers Ltd

First published in Great Britain by Pen Press

All paper used in the printing of this book has been made from wood grown in managed, sustainable forests.

ISBN13: 978-1-906710-32-3

Printed and bound in the UK
by Cpod Trowbridge, Wiltshire
Pen Press is an imprint of Indepenpress Publishing Limited
25 Eastern Place
Brighton
BN2 1GJ

A catalogue record of this book is available from
the British Library

Cover design by Jacqueline Abromeit

About the Author

Don Moggs, now in his 87th year, was born in London's East End and started school there. In the later twenties the family moved to the new council estate in Dagenham. Some years later they moved to Brentwood, following his father's job. At fifteen Don finds himself in Enfield, which just after his move there, the story begins.

Previous publications:

Chapter One

School – The Final Years

Don walked slowly down the platform and boarded the waiting train. It would be five minutes before it was due to leave and he sat back in an empty compartment facing the engine and opened his case. He took out homework from the previous night and scanned it for possible errors, soon returning it to the case and, sitting back, looked out of the window, thinking. Very few people had boarded the train and those he saw had walked past and found compartments further along. The train started, slowly pulling the eight carriages from the station and on towards London. As they left the station he glanced across the allotments to the house he had just left, their new house, a terraced house in a road not far from the station and shops. It had three bedrooms, an outside toilet but no bathroom, the galvanised bath hung on a hook outside which he could see from the train.

They had only just moved in and Don did not like it one bit, especially as he would now have a very long journey to school and had had to leave all the friends he had made where he used to live. He understood why they had moved, his dad and mum had both come from Enfield and their parents were getting old and may need some help, so dad, who was an engine driver, had asked for a transfer from his depot at Brentwood in Essex to the depot at Enfield. Don's journey to school would now take him up to Liverpool Street where he would change trains to go on to the station in Essex near to his school. The train up to London, (people who lived in the suburbs always used to say 'going up to London', although to most outsiders they already lived in London), would stop at all fourteen stations and then

Don would have to cross over to the other side of the vast terminus to catch another slow train out to Gidea Park in Essex. His dad had bought him a season ticket but because it was at a special rate, he being a railwayman's son, it was third class, unlike all ordinary season tickets at that time, which were issued as second class. This did not worry Don as he had been used to travelling third class for almost four years on the previous short train journeys he had taken to school, and indeed starting in earlier days when just eleven most of his friends had joined him in third class in order to play 'carriage he' or have races over the tops of the seats. Indeed, when he had passed the stage of such childish things, they had continued to support him over the years in the old 'cattle trucks' which had separate compartments but low backs to the seats so it was possible to climb over the seats and below the luggage rack into the next compartment.

Nearing the junction at Bethnal Green he casually looked out of the window at St Paul's Cathedral and then as the train turned the bend, which the passenger could not feel, he turned his head to the window on the other side of the carriage and there, as his dad had told him years ago, was the cathedral again. He, of course, understood now how it happened but as a young child visiting his grandparents it had always puzzled him and it happened as if by magic. Of course he would not have to go by train to visit his grandparents now as they lived in the same town, and he would not now have to suffer the cold nights waiting on Bethnal Green station when they often changed trains to go out to where they used to live.

The train pulled slowly into platform 2 at the terminus and Don made his way across the footbridges to platform 16 and his waiting train. By studying the timetables Don had seen that certain trains would miss some of the stations, like first stop Ilford, but this particular one would stop at every one; stations with names such as Coburn Road, Seven Kings, Goodmayes, Stratford, where he had been born, and Forest Gate where he had started school when they had lived in the East End before moving out to Dagenham. In all, some twelve stations. My goodness, Don thought to himself, twenty-six stations to school and on steam trains which could hardly get up speed before they came to the next station!

About forty-five minutes later he was getting out at Gidea Park with other boys who had boarded the train at Chadwell Heath, the Dagenham boys who came from the big LCC estate, and Romford, those whose parents were likely middle class and buying their own house. Don had been a Dagenham scholarship boy when he had started at the school and he had noticed how different the boys were from Romford and from the local area around the school. For one thing they talked without the East End accent of those from Dagenham and they appeared to be snobbish, many of them being fee-paying pupils, and Don sensed they wondered who on earth were these ruffians who talked differently from them. It did not last too long as Don had soon become friends with many, due possibly to his ability at football and the fact that he could look after himself in the ring – boxing being all they seemed to do in the gym as the master had been an amateur middleweight champion himself and the Head was all for the sport being taught to all the boys. Nevertheless, throughout his four years at the school the cross mixing between Dagenham and Gidea Park/Romford boys was rare.

Walking along the platform he joined some of his friends and they walked on the short-cut path to the school as if it were an ordinary day, others quite oblivious to the fact that he had travelled so far and for so long that morning.

"What's on the programme for today?" one asked.

"We start with double maths," said another.

"Oh gawd – I suppose old McTravers will do his usual," Don said and the others laughed gleefully.

Ten minutes later after a very brief assembly they made their way to the classroom. Don went to his usual seat in the corner on the same side as the door and the general hubbub faded as the chap nearest the door said, "Cave."

This was it, Don thought, and true enough in burst McTravers, his gown billowing out behind and without turning his head thrust his arm sideways and pointing to Don's corner, whilst still making his way to his desk, shouted, "Moggs," at this, everybody turned their heads to look back at Don, "What's the cube root of 125?"

Don hesitated and grinned back at the many faces looking at him, some trying to make him laugh whilst others tried to mouth the answer. "Wake up, Moggs, you look half asleep."

"Five, Sir, and yes I am tired, been on trains since seven this morning."

"Pity your parents couldn't remember you had got to go to school, where have you been?"

"I have been travelling from home, we have moved house to north London, Enfield in fact."

"Good god, boy, you can't travel all that way every day and expect to do a good day's work."

"I have to do it for this term since we're taking the School Certificate – after that I don't know."

"All right, everybody, settle down and turn to page 220."

He had just said this when a soft knock came on the door and in came a fourth-former.

"What is it, boy?"

"Mr Schofield wants Burns to report to the gym."

Everyone in the class knew what this meant. Schofield was the gym master and with permission of the Head he ran a boxing tournament and every boy, all 600 of them, had to enter and could be called out of any class at any time.

Burns, a timid fifth-former, rose from his chair and made his way to the door past grinning classmates and with McTravers smiling as he passed him wished him luck and hoped he would be able to come back after he had been to First Aid. At this there was general laughter through the class.

Half an hour later Burns returned with a decidedly red nose and a slight swelling under one eye.

"I hope he looks as bad as you, Burns," McTravers chirped.

4

Maths was followed by Geography, which was Don's favourite subject and the only one in which he excelled – old Elwood certainly knew how to teach and keep your interest, Don thought, not like the Doctor. Don hated Latin and although Dr Witt had obviously taken a liking to him, he was not able to get him to learn the subject. Why he was a favourite he didn't know, perhaps the Doc felt sorry for him. I don't want anyone feeling sorry for me, I can look after myself, he had often thought, mind you some might start to feel sorry for him now, and with just reason since he had to travel so far to school.

The day ended uneventfully and Don was soon on a train heading for London. He felt sleepy and started to nod off but shook himself awake. Supposing I fell asleep and they left me in the train at Liverpool Street, I could end up anywhere, he thought, they ought to have little cards you could pin above your head which said, 'Wake me up at Stratford' or some other place you wanted to be woken up. But supposing you were in a compartment on your own, it wouldn't work then, he pondered.

Liverpool Street at five o'clock was beginning to get busy and he passed scores of people changing platforms across the bridges. He glanced up at the indicators in front of platforms 1 and 2 and noted the next train to Enfield was from no.1 at 5.20, just a few minutes to wait and this one was going fast to Hackney Downs; that's better, he thought. The train was already fairly full and he tried to find one of the few non-smoking compartments but all were full, so he seated himself in one of the others with five men who did not appear to be smoking at the time. He wondered if he should look at his homework for tonight, but his mind was too unsettled and so he stared outside the carriage window at the people walking along the platform. Some men with bowler hats, pinstripe trousers and black jackets, and of course the obligatory rolled umbrella, some in smart office suits and others in overalls and wearing caps. The few women passing were mostly young girls since most older women in those days stayed at home. Here he was, fifteen years old, and still at school whereas some of these girls were younger than him, had left school and now worked in the City, as his sister had done a few years back when she had also left school at fourteen.

The train was now beginning to fill up fast and a few workmen got into his compartment and immediately started smoking, how he hated it, many times at home there had been trouble over his dad smoking when others were having a meal, yes his mother knew how much he hated it. At that moment a whistle sounded and people started running and there was much slamming of doors, which reminded him of the story his mother had told him of her day out with Dad in London last week. He chuckled to himself as he remembered. She had told him how they had got on the wrong train on this very platform. She said they walked over to the platforms for Enfield when suddenly Dad grabbed her hand and almost pulled her through the gate on to the platform and bundled her into the train just before it pulled out from the station. Almost immediately, his mother said, Dad somehow knew something was wrong. "We're on a carriage train," he said, "We've done it now, this train will go right through to Enfield or Chingford without stopping." "I like that," she said, "*we've* done it! I'm still out of breath from you pulling me onto the platform."

Now a carriage train, for those of you who do not know, was what the railwaymen called trains that were not carrying passengers but were heading for a depot or sidings or anywhere, known only to the driver and the signalman. It seems his dad, who should have known better, seeing a train by the platform had opened the purposely-closed gate and rushed through without checking the indicators or appreciating there was no ticket collector at the barrier. His mother, telling the story, had a job to stop laughing as she recalled that her husband had said they would now have to duck down every time they passed a station, as he did not want his mates to see him. She said of course he knew when they were coming to a station and told her to get ready to duck and as they got to the platform he said, "Duck", so they both bent down so that anyone on the platforms could not see them. This went on until the train eventually stopped at Chingford and with no one on the platform they were able to alight without, so they believed, anyone noticing them. From there they had to catch a train back to Hackney Downs Junction and so connect with a train going to their destination, Enfield. Whether in fact the driver or his fireman saw them, Don never found out but he knew his dad would hardly have been the one anyone would have dared say anything about it to his face.

Don's train started up and was soon rattling through Cambridge Heath, having passed Bethnal Green in a leisurely manner. The next station he recalled would be London Fields and he remembered that as a young child it had always puzzled him why London Fields was farther away from London than Cambridge Heath when Cambridge was miles outside London. A few more people squeezed in at Hackney Downs, then came the stopping and starting for the rest of the journey. Rectory Road, Stamford Hill and Seven Sisters were soon reached, the latter he recalled was where you took the little train on the short journey to Palace Gates, the station for Alexandra Palace where the single-deck trams ran up to the palace – 'broken trams' he had been told he had called them, when young, since the only trams he knew, which at that time ran all over London, had a second deck. Then on to Bruce Grove and White Hart Lane, where his dad had taken him once or twice to see the Spurs. Next Silver Street, Lower Edmonton, Bush Hill Park and finally Enfield. Don had managed to keep awake the whole journey but he was glad to get into the fresh air out of the smoky compartment. He was soon walking behind the big ABC cinema to the path which led to the back of his new home, the sun was still shining and he was pleased he would not likely have to do this journey in the winter. It was getting on for half-past six when he entered the house. His sister was already home from work and tea was ready. His first day of what would be his final term at that school was over.

Chapter Two

Over the next few weeks Don's journeys to school were largely uneventful. He began to see the same faces on the trains and on the platforms – the red-faced man who boarded the train regularly at Stratford always got out at Romford, then there was the young girl going to school who got in at Chadwell Heath and got out at the next station, Romford. Don had begun to take an interest in girls and when one day she got into his carriage he was tempted to speak, but he never did. Going back home at night he sometimes managed to catch a fast train which stopped only about four times up to the City, but the advantage gained was always lost at Liverpool Street when he invariably had to wait for the same train to Enfield.

His days at school continued as before, he was now in the fifth form and would be taking the General School Certificate, or Matric as it was sometimes called. Don knew he would have difficulty in doing well, he had for the last few years always been near the bottom of the class and now with the long journey he never did feel much like working hard at school and certainly not when he got home at night. He was one of the youngest in the class, some boys being almost a year older than him. The only thing he shone at in his time at that school was football and boxing, both of which he had now finished with – football because it was summer term and boxing because the finals for the year had taken place the previous term and the new round of contests had only just begun and since he had not been called he guessed old Schofield was waiting to see if he would be there next term; Don had been in the finals most terms.

He missed going home on the train with friends, who he now hardly ever saw at school as they were in different classes.

He remembered the fun they had had, especially a few years back, but now of course he was past the young age when he and others would wait on the platform when the train started and then run alongside to see who would be last to board, whilst the porter shouted and threatened to tell the school – although he never did. Indeed there was not much fun in travelling now, in fact none at all. He often used to think of a few years back when they had races over the top of the seats and that one special occasion when he was racing, and winning, when coming to the end of the carriage and running into Romford station he dropped into the end compartment, which he thought was empty, only to find seated in the corner another passenger – a big boy. The boy Don had beaten in the race peeped over the top of the compartment and immediately made a hasty exit onto the platform of the station the train had just stopped at. The boy sitting quietly in the corner turned out to be from Don's school and after lecturing him about what he had been doing, gave him a hundred lines. Don duly did these when he got home, without telling his dad what they were for, and handed them in to the lad the next day – it was some year or so later when he discovered that the boy was only a third-former at the time and of course could not give out lines. He and his friends must have had a good laugh over it, as he did later.

Although school, football and boxing were important in Don's life he was not ignorant of what was going on around him. His dad usually bought a *Daily Herald* newspaper and Don would read it at night, he read not only the sport but also took a keen interest in the major happenings in the world. He particularly keenly followed the progress of the Spanish Civil War and studied the maps that showed the position of opposing forces almost on a daily basis. He read of the atrocities committed by both sides and failed to understand how people could be so cruel. His particular interest in this war had been heightened by how last year it had affected him.

He often ran through it in his mind as he watched the many stations on his journey to school come and go. Early the previous year, 1936, the school had announced a summer cruise under the Secondary School Travel Trust and Don had taken home the leaflet for his parents to see. He had not expected any interest would be shown, as he had never known any of his friends from Dagenham going on one of these yearly holidays. Much to his surprise his dad asked him if he would like to go and taken completely by surprise he had said he would. The cost would be six guineas for a two-week cruise and of course he would need some spending money. Six guineas (£6.30p in today's money) sounds very little, but to a working man in those days it was a great deal. It was more than his dad earned in a week and was as much as three weeks' money to the average manual worker. Anyway his parents decided he could go and he later found out that they had decided to forego going anywhere on the one week's paid holiday his dad would get that year. Don was of course pleased to be going but did not realise at the time the sacrifice his parents were making for him.

The itinerary for the cruise was Southampton, Lisbon, Gibraltar, Ceuta, Casablanca and Madeira, and added to this came the prospect of meeting an uncle in a foreign country. The latter came about when the family visited his dad's brother, who lived in one of the new and, to Charlie, very posh houses being built north-west of London for about £500. Like Don's dad, Uncle Vic was an engine driver, but he now drove engines in Nigeria having taken up a lucrative offer made by Nigerian Railways a few years earlier. To Don his cousin Allan and his friends, whom he met on one of the many building sites when the family had visited his uncle, were lucky rich boys. At the time of their visit his uncle was nearing the end of six months' leave and would be leaving shortly for another eighteen months in Nigeria. When Don's dad told his brother that Don was going on a cruise and was asked when this would be, it was soon discovered their ships would be due to call in to

Madeira at the same time. The possibility of meeting his uncle in a foreign country of course made the cruise even more exciting, but little did he know then that the plan to meet might be thwarted by a development in another country.

On the long journey to school Don tried many times to study but invariably started to feel sleepy so instead he would try and read other passengers' papers or just let his mind wander over past events. He remembered the time when just before the date for departure for the cruise he was required to go to the school during the holidays to meet the Headmaster who wanted to speak to the boys going on the overseas adventure. It was for Don the first time he had seen what really rich people spent some of their money on. When he arrived at school on this visit most of the others had seen the Head and he and one other were the last two to present themselves. They were asked to go to the Head's house in the grounds of the school where he would see them. Don and the other lad duly knocked at the door and were ushered upstairs to a bedroom, by a maid, where the Head was sitting up in bed – he was unwell. Don never remembered what was said but what did stick in his mind was the carpet on the floor. There were no carpets in his house at home and the soft, fluffy white one that covered the floor fascinated him. He had never seen anything like it and it made a lasting impression on him. Oh yes, he had seen better houses on the films but they were all in black and white and in any case were not real, or at least to Don they were only in films, but now he had seen it for himself, and all in colour. What it must be like to be rich, he had pondered.

By the time one morning the train passed Coburn Road station his story of the cruise was up to the day when he was due to depart. Yes that was it, he thought, Mum and Dad took me up to Waterloo station to catch the boat train to Southampton and after we boarded the ship, HMS *Dilwara*, all of us were given a card to post home. The card contained information on a revised itinerary – the ship would not be calling at Gibraltar or Ceuta! He remembered the big

11

disappointment of all concerned and how they were told that this was due to trouble that was starting up in Spain. A General Franco, a name since known by all in Britain and in the papers daily, but then just a name, in command of thousands of troops in Spanish Morocco had declared against the then government of Spain and was sending his troops across from Ceuta to Algeciras to take control of Spain. The British Navy, with a large presence in Gibraltar, he remembered being told, had been advised by the British government to close the Straits to all shipping whilst the 'invasion' was taking place, in order to avoid any incident which might occur if action were taken against the invading ships. It was this that had begun his keen interest in what turned out to be the start of the Spanish Civil War.

Don's thoughts were interrupted when an argument broke out between two men sitting on the other side of the compartment; what it was over Don didn't know, but they nearly got to blows when another passenger intervened and pointed out there was a young schoolboy in the compartment. There was no mistake Don was a schoolboy, as when going to school he always wore his school cap. He had noticed that one of the two men who had been arguing was bigger than the other and Don's mind went back to his dad's advice, "Don't let any big bully push you around, if you can't punch them, kick 'em – the bigger they are the harder they fall." His dad knew what to do, Don knew, because he had told him that during the last war he had had gloves on with Bombardier Billy Wells the British Heavyweight Champion, and in Don's mind he could see this man banging the big gong at the beginning of some of the films he saw at the cinema.

That evening, over tea, he told his mother of the altercation on the train and it reminded him that at the time he had in his mind been going through the story of the cruise. He then remembered the photos he had taken whilst away.

"Mum, you know the photos I took on the cruise, do you know where they are?"

"Look in the top drawer of the cabinet in your room, I think I put them in there when we moved in. If I had left them to you to bring they would still be back in Brentwood."

Don laughed and thanked her. So after tea he went upstairs and found them, just where his mother had thought they were. In the small Selo packet were the small black and white photos he had taken with his dad's Ensign box camera and underneath the photos was a school magazine in which one of the masters had had Don's story of the cruise printed. He looked through the photos and recalled what happened at the three ports his ship called at. Yes, the Spanish Civil War was responsible for spoiling the cruise – well hardly spoiling but he would have liked to have gone to Gibraltar as then he could say he had been to Spain, well not quite, but almost. Of course some of the boys would have been going on a trip to Malaga from Gibraltar but not Don, it was an extra that Don didn't like to ask his parents to pay for. He didn't mind missing Ceuta, in Spanish Morocco, as he guessed it would have been somewhat like Casablanca in French Morocco, but he would have liked to say he had been to Spain, particularly as he had at school taken a keen interest in the Peninsular War, and he knew Gibraltar was part of the Peninsular. He continued browsing through the small bundle of photos and came to those taken of Funchal harbour which reminded him of how after all he had met his uncle. Don had not remembered whether the date his uncle was due there would now be the same as the time Don's ship would be there since the itinerary had been changed. However, it must have been the same for on the first morning after they arrived in the harbour he had been down washing below deck when some of his friends came rushing in to say a man in a white suit was up on deck asking for him. Don tore up to the deck and there was Uncle Vic resplendent in a white suit and wearing a topee. His ship, one of the Elder Dempster liners, had anchored that morning in the bay and his uncle had boarded a tender and had come over to see if he could find his nephew. Uncle took him up to the First Class area on the Promenade deck where only teachers and a few parents were allowed and they sat and talked. He remembered how important his uncle looked and he smiled to think he was an engine driver, just like his dad, when he looked like a great white hunter. Of course in Nigeria all engine drivers were white and were very highly respected, having two black firemen to work with them, and he had heard his uncle tell his dad that he hardly ever got his hands dirty as drivers did in England. Anyway, after showing him around the First Class area, everyone acknowledging his uncle as they passed, uncle had asked if Don would like some of his friends to come with him over to the town. So he collected three others and uncle soon hailed a tender to take them over to the shore where they all had tea, or perhaps it was coffee, he couldn't remember, and cakes, all paid for by his uncle. His uncle's ship left that evening to call next at Las Palmas in the Canary Islands.

Among the photos were one or two of Casablanca where he remembered some of the boys, himself amongst them, went with a guide into the Arab quarter, which their master had strictly forbidden them to do. He then opened the school magazine and read the article he had written and looked at the newspaper he had bought in Casablanca with the front page full of the story of 800 English boys arriving in town. Yes it was quite a memory to have, a good memory except for being seasick soon after getting out of the hammock in which he slept! His Majesty's troopship *Dilwara* would always be remembered. In later years Don always said he had been in Casablanca before Humphrey Bogart!

Of course there were other events that brought headlines to the newspapers, besides the war in Spain, and one morning whilst travelling up to Liverpool St on his way to school he was shocked to read on other passengers' papers the headlines which read, 'Jean Harlow Dies' or 'Blonde Bombshell Dies'. Don had seen her on a couple of occasions in films and had instantly taken a liking to her, in fact it had been one of his party pieces a few years earlier to shout a few words in the manner of this lady. She was only twenty-six but had made a name for herself all over the Western world. Film stars in the thirties were the most well-known people, particularly those from Hollywood, and the news of the death of such a famous person made headlines and became the topic of conversation by all ages.

By carefully reading other passengers' papers, hopefully without them noticing, he thus was able to keep right up with the news. He noticed that most passengers, at least those in the third-class compartments in which he travelled, read the *Herald*, his dad's paper, or the *Chronicle*. It was rare to see the *Daily Mail* and he never remembered seeing the *Times* or *Telegraph* except when held open by men in pinstriped trousers whilst waiting for a train, nearly always of course carrying their obligatory umbrella in one hand and entering the first or second-class compartments when the train arrived. The *Daily Herald* reminded him of how a few years back his parents had got him a full set of encyclopaedias by collecting tokens from that newspaper and sending these together with half a crown (2s 6d or 12½p in today's money) to obtain three books at a time. There were twelve in all – ten encyclopaedias and two dictionaries. Don spent hours reading these, particularly anything to do with geography and history, and soon became quite familiar with many countries in the world and their populations. Population figures seemed to remain in his mind more than most things and he found he was able to quote populations of towns all over Britain, which he had gathered from the treasured books that quoted the census of 1930. Of course years later this became a useless piece of information as it all changed – London, then the largest city in the world, was destined not to come in the top ten as far as population was concerned, but when Don was young he could impress people with his off-the-cuff knowledge.

Don, now fifteen, had pocket money and shortly after starting his long journey to school his dad had increased this to half a crown a week which he spent most of going to the pictures. There were three cinemas in his new home town with the ABC his favourite, then the Rialto, the second best, and the Queens which he avoided going to unless there was a really good film he wanted to see. Although he was a big lad he sometimes had to wait outside before he could get in if the picture had an adult stamp on it, when he would have to ask people if they would take his money and buy a ticket for him. Most people didn't seem to mind but some did, whilst there were others who pointed out they were going to the more expensive seats in the circle or at the back. The ABC certainly gave you the best value for money – for sixpence Don could see two big films, the news, a cartoon and then a stage show, and of course the organ. Four hours of entertainment for sixpence!

At weekends he would often go out for rides on his bike or go for a walk round the new and unfamiliar streets, or visit his Auntie Grace and Uncle Charlie who lived not far from him in Bush Hill Park. Their son Harry was just over a year younger than Don and quite unlike him in many ways. Harry did not seem to have many friends when at home and his mother was obviously keen for Harry to become friendly with Don. He discovered they both liked walking and so decided to meet for a walk one Sunday morning. The Sunday walk was successful and it was soon to become a weekly affair and in fact carried on for well over two years.

It was at this time that Don found the local park and spent time going there, watching the cricket or kicking a ball around.

Chapter Three

The summer term of '37 passed slowly, with skies mostly blue and little rain. Don, always an early riser, found no difficulty in getting to the station early for the long journey to school but by the end of the journey home he was invariably tired. Homework was neglected and although he tried his best to do revision on the train he knew he was slipping backwards.

Eventually the examinations came and he did no better than he had expected. The results would not be known until after the term had ended. There was no farewell from his friends when the last day arrived as they said they would see him on the day the results would be shown on the school notice board in the holidays. He dreaded the thought of that day, as he feared the worse. What would happen if he failed? It was usual for boys to seek work immediately at the end of the fifth year, the time the School Certificate Examinations were taken. Sometimes boys stayed on in the sixth form until they got a job or, very rarely, studied for the Higher Schools Examination, which would give them an opportunity for a better job or perhaps an opportunity to go to a university. Don never knew anyone who went or tried to go to university, quite unlike today when it seems it is the exception not to go. The only universities he had ever heard of were Oxford and Cambridge and this was entirely due to the boat race, which in those days had a significance far greater than it has today. He never gave a thought as to who went to those universities, but if asked he would probably have guessed they must be wealthy people who came from expensive schools, the public schools like Eton and Harrow of which he had heard. Nearly everyone Don knew in the thirties left school at fourteen and started work, the only exception being that minority who went to a grammar school or their equivalent, when one generally left at sixteen, although even there some boys would leave to start work at fourteen.

Since he was younger than most in his year at school he would not be sixteen until the following year and thus his parents made enquiries at the local grammar school in his new town to see if they would take him if it were decided he should continue his schooling. One day he was given an interview at the new school, Enfield Grammar, and in turn they contacted his present school and in due time he was offered a place at the new school that his mum and dad decided he take in order, if necessary, to take the Matric again or at least until he got a job if the results from the examinations just taken were good.

The day for getting the results duly arrived and he made the long journey once more to see what he had done. He found many happy faces around the notice board when he eventually arrived and squeezed through to look for himself. He had failed! It was really no more than he had expected but it still hurt, especially as there were so many of his friends who had passed, even Pip Grover who always managed to come below him in class had got a pass – it wasn't fair, he thought, certainly banging his other elbow when he hit one, to avoid disappointment his mum had told him years ago, did not seem to have worked. He hastily said goodbye to some of his friends and made his way back to the station. He was wondering what his parents might say when he got home, after all they had supported him for over a year longer than his sister and he felt so guilty that he would probably have to continue at school to try and get the School Certificate. He knew unemployment was high, many people out of work, three million he had heard, nearly all men as very few married women went to work in those days. It certainly would be difficult finding work, doubly so since he had been educated at a grammar school and it was expected therefore he would get an office job – a job with a pension, his dad would say, "Don't go on the railway, son, nor in a factory doing manual work, get yourself a good office job." But without the school certificate it would be hard.

When he arrived home both his parents were there; his dad was on nights and was preparing to go to work.

"I failed," Don said and paused, "I'm so sorry," he said.

His dad was the first to speak.

"Never mind, son, you did your best. You'll do better next time. Here," he put his hand in his pocket and fished out a coin, "take yourself to the pictures."

Don was never to forget this episode in his life. In later years he wondered whether perhaps his parents were not expecting him to pass, they knew he had not done so well in class over the past two years and with the long journey to and from school, which was no fault of his own, they maybe thought his work could have suffered. But at the time it never entered his head, he just knew this was the kindest thing anyone had ever done for him in his life and he would never forget it.

Chapter Four

There were still four weeks to go before he was due to start at the new school and when he had finished any household chores he would spend the remainder of the day over the park or on his bicycle. When going to the park he invariably took his football, as then he knew he would surely find someone to play with, as not too many boys were lucky enough to have a proper ball to kick about. One day in the park he met a friendly chap about his age who seemed to like to play in goal, which suited Don well as he could practise his shots. Mac, Don never did ask him his first name, was at the same school that Don would soon be joining, and after that first day the two of them met regularly. Of course the goal they used was only two coats, which meant there was always much running behind to collect the ball when a goal was scored or a shot missed the goal. A Ronnie Vale, who Don learnt had had trials for the Spurs, later joined Mac and Don and the three spent many mornings happily kicking the ball around. Sometimes in the early summer evenings he returned to the park because impromptu games were set up with two goals and at first by hanging around on the edge he knew he would soon manage to get a game. In those days you went "Pudding and Beef" with some other boy waiting for a game, then another boy who had assumed captaincy of one side called either "pudding" or "beef" to pick the teams. After seeing how Don played, on some evenings there were arguments over which side he joined. "We'll have ginger" or "We'll have ginna" was the cry. It was a good time for Don and he began to like his new home and soon forgot the many friends he had had where he used to live.

One morning while kicking a ball about with Mac, a big fellow, Ernie, who although only having slippers on his feet had a kick like a mule, joined them. Ernie, like Mac, was at the school Don would be joining and Mac confirmed big Ernie played for the school first team.

Thus the remainder of the holiday passed with Don making many new friends and gaining a reputation amongst the local lads as good at football.

At home they soon had an addition to the house. One of his uncles came to live with them. It was a tight squeeze in their three-bedroom terraced house but it made no difference to Don, in fact he liked having his uncle in the house as he was interested in football and brought an evening paper home every night when he came home from work. Don guessed his uncle was doing quite well to be able to buy a paper every evening. Unfortunately, his uncle was ill, he had great difficulty in breathing. He worked as an engineer for the Post Office and had, as his dad had told him, been a 'time serving'[1] man in the army. Don was impressed too by being told Uncle Trait used to be able to run a hundred yards in even time (ten seconds), in those days almost international standard.

The day for joining the new school arrived and Don was allocated to a class who would be taking the School Certificate Examinations the following year. Since he had been studying some different subjects from those taken by the new school, he learnt he would be allowed to study much of his time on his own. It was during one such period on his own near lunchtime on the first day that a boy told him he was wanted in the masters' common room. He couldn't think what he was wanted for, and as he had never been inside such a room he was a little apprehensive. He presented himself and was immediately joined by a man who introduced himself as the sports master.

---

[1] A phrase used at the time to mean a regular soldier that had served a long time, usually this meant at least 21 years.

21

"Ernie Salmon tells me you play good football. He says you have a cannonball shot. Tell me about yourself and what position and teams you played for at your last school."

Don related his experience and the master told him that if he would like to play for the school he would give him a run out in the second eleven the following Saturday. He told Don that the school had a good reputation as a football school and ran four teams, the same as his previous school. He was told where to collect his shirt and that the ground was near the junior school a few hundred yards up the road. His first match would be a home fixture.

Football meant a lot to Don and he was proud that on his first day he had been given a chance to play the next Saturday. It was the first thing he told his parents when he got home, at least he was not a complete failure. His dad said he would come along to watch and Uncle, who had earlier been told of Don being quite good at football, said he too would be along to his first game.

For those of you who do not know, the senior part of Enfield Grammar School was situated in the middle of the town next to the market square and parish church. The buildings next to the square date back to Tudor times when the school was founded. The junior school was in a country house about a quarter of a mile away and housed the gym and changing rooms for football, the pitches being in the adjoining grounds.

The first game of the second eleven was against Tollington school and turned out to be very one-sided with the Grammar ending up 11-0 winners, with Don scoring 4 and having a hand in most of the others. Everyone congratulated him on his performance and it was widely said that he should be in the first eleven. Members of the family, including his uncle, became regular visitors for the home games. Don was beginning to like being at the new school and it soon reflected in his class work.

He had never previously liked school very much, probably because he had found much of the work at his last school a little difficult. He had enjoyed the sport, which, apart from boxing, football and cricket, included road running. The latter because his school was in a built-up area and they could hardly have cross-country races with no country. These runs always turned into races for the first twenty or so better runners and Don, although never coming first, recollected he never came below fifth and was often second in the almost weekly run which was invariably won by the same boy, Woollard.

Naturally on the first day at the new school he had been somewhat concerned, but on learning he could work a lot on his own and then getting the boost from the sports master and his subsequent success at his first few games, he wondered whether perhaps it would not be so bad after all.

Chapter Five

Thus a new episode in his life began, a time to be looked back on in later years as one of the happiest of his life. He continued to score goals for the second eleven and the House and after a few weeks turned out for the first eleven and scored five goals in his first match which they won 14-1! In schoolwork he could do no wrong, and all the things which he did not understand at his last school were suddenly becoming clear. The atmosphere in the class was quite different from that he had experienced previously and instead of being the butt of one or two masters, who so obviously wanted to impress the others pupils, he became the bright boy of the class and received praise all round. Was it the fact that he was now more in his own age group than he had been before, or was it the relaxed atmosphere of the school? Whatever it was, everything seemed to click into place.

One Saturday, later in the season, his uncle took him to the Spurs, which was a short train journey from Enfield Town station. But it took them a long while to walk to the ground from White Hart Lane station as it was not easy for his uncle to walk, having every so often to stop to catch his breath. It was even worse walking back from the station in Enfield and they had to stop several times in the short distance to their home.

Don liked his uncle and they became good friends. He had obviously been quite a handsome well-built man when he was young but now he was looking drawn and older than his years. Sadly it was not many months after coming to live with them that he had to be taken into hospital. Don went to see him there, and it was the first time he had seen a dying man and found it difficult to know what to say to his uncle. The memory of this kind man, a friend, lying still in his bed was to remain with him always. He died a few days later, he was not yet fifty.

It was not long after this that his dad's mother died and it was apparently agreed that Don's granddad was to come to live with them. Granddad, who had also been an engine driver, was now retired but although doing manual work all his life had somehow acquired some money.

Don's dad told him his father used to do the "gee gees". Don himself had never had a bet on a horse and of course had never been to a horse race but was not ignorant of betting on horses. He had more than once taken pieces of paper with money folded inside to a house opposite to where his grandfather lived. Betting other than on a course was illegal at that time and children were often used to carry the bets to the undercover bookmaker or his runner. Don himself also regularly marked the race meetings in the daily papers and when the results were given out in the news on the wireless in the evening he would look at how he had done. It was then not unusual to see the racing section of the paper marked with many first, second and thirds and Don knew that if he had betted he would have done very well for himself. But whether granddad had got his money that way Don was not sure.

However, his parents and granddad were soon looking for a new house to move to and much to Don's surprise he found they were to move a mile or so away to a posh road, one of the best in the Enfield area. The house was to be rented, although Don later found out that granddad had offered to buy it. However, his mother was too proud to accept the gesture or, as his sister told him, she did not want to be obligated in any way.

The day came when they moved and Don saw the house for the first time. To him it was really posh. It had four bedrooms and a bathroom, so no more bathing in front of the fire on a Friday night, and although terraced it had a small garage built under, what turned out to be, his bedroom. As far as he could see it was the only garage in the street and later he was to meet for the first time a person who owned a car, the car that was in their garage, which the man had been renting from the previous occupants and was to continue as his parents' tenant.

Don's reputation as a footballer was well established and his house master, assuming he could run too, asked him if he would run for the house in the annual cross-country race to be held shortly. Thus he entered. He was told the race was run in the grounds of a big country house just north of the town in the village of Forty Hill. He knew his mother had lived in that village when a child and when he told her where the race would take place she hesitated before answering and he noticed a faraway look come into her eyes.

"What's a matter, Mum?"

"Oh it's nothing. I hope you do well."

"What do you mean nothing? Don't you want me to run?"

"Of course I do. It is just that I know the house well and it brought back memories."

"How do you know it, Mum?"

"When I was young we were very poor, my father was ill and had not long to live. Mother went out cleaning when she could find the work but we had hardly any money. The man who owned the house you are talking about, in those days was a Colonel Bowles, and he allowed any poor children in the village to go to the kitchen to get soup and bread. So when we came out of school at dinnertime and when I thought my friends were not looking, I used to sneak in through the gates of the big house and go round to the kitchen where the cook used to give me a good feed."

"I don't suppose we will go near the house, it seems the Grammar have been allowed to run their cross-country race over the grounds for a number of years."

"I don't know anything about that. Anyway I'll make sure you have a good meal at dinnertime on the day of the race. You'll need it running over all those fields."

The day of the race came and Don went home to his dinner and to collect his shorts and plimsolls. On the occasions he did go home midday he usually only had a snack but on this day his mother had cooked a meat pudding, potatoes and cabbage. He wasn't so sure he should have a second helping but meat pudding was his favourite and his mum said he ought to have something substantial for the run. He cycled back to school and was there in time to go with others on their bikes for the ride to Forty Hill.

When he arrived at the starting point it looked as if most of the six hundred pupils at the school had made the journey to watch. Fortunately it was a bright day and the juniors whose race was first had soon taken off their jackets and were ready to run. The course for them was slightly shorter and it was not too long before a white speck appeared over the crest of a hill followed soon after by others. A run for the line amid great applause and the favourite had won.

Then Don lined up with the eighty or so senior runners and at the whistle blown by the sports master the race was on. There seemed to be an extra spurt at the beginning and Don had a job to keep near the front. It soon became obvious why a sprint at the start when at the end of the first field the runners had to squeeze through a fence in single file. Most, if not all except of course Don, had run the race in earlier years and once he got through the fence he knew he would have to speed up if he wanted to get up towards the leaders. Over a fence and then a stile followed by a ploughed field and he was going well, passing runners all the time. Two or three more fields with markers giving directions to ensure runners went the right way and soon he found he was on his own but ahead with a marker telling him he was third. Suddenly ahead he spotted two figures going through a hedge. He recognised one as being his friend Bob, who he knew ran regularly to keep fit, and the other was a fellow who had been pointed out to him as being an older boy who ran for the county. Don knew that he could not catch those two who must be the leaders so he ran steadily, assured by a marker that he was near the end. Suddenly another runner caught him up and as they were both in the same house they decided to run in together, hoping to gain an extra point for the house. Thus Don and his housemate ran in third but were told each would be counted three and a half, so no extra points gained for the house. The house captain, masters and many others present congratulated him, all agreeing he had done remarkably well not having run the course before.

No, it did not seem that anything could go wrong for him in his time at the Grammar. He was made Vice-Captain of the first eleven football and then became Captain when the previous captain left the school to start work. He became a prefect, got his school colours and was made House Captain, all in a period of eighteen months. He also took the School Certificate examinations and succeeded in getting exemption from Matriculation with a special prize awarded for his geography paper. He could, it seemed, do no wrong.

Soon after he had arrived at the new school he had become quite friendly with one particular lad in his class. This boy was extremely popular with all, good at boxing, football and running. He was also well up in current affairs and Don enjoyed talking to him. It was during 1937 and 38 that many things happening on the continent were taking the headlines away from events at home. The Spanish Civil War raged on with Franco and his supporters gaining ground. Madrid was, however, still held by the government helped by the International Brigade, made up of left wing volunteers from many countries, and while this city remained in the hands of the left, Franco could not finally claim control of Spain. The papers Don read were obviously sympathetic to the Spanish government forces and the exploits of a British sea captain who ran the blockade of the Spanish Navy, supporting Franco, to bring food to the north, excited Don's imagination. The sea captain used the port of Santander and was dubbed 'Potato Jones' by the press. In Germany, Adolph Hitler was flexing his muscles and sent troops into the Rhineland, which had been forbidden under the Treaty of Versailles; he was also giving help to Franco in Spain by allocating part of the Lufwaffe to him. Russia on the other hand was giving material help to the

Spanish government. Mussolini was also making loud boasts that were repeated from time to time in the press.

Then in 1938 Hitler 'annexed' Austria, a move that was popular with many if not most Austrians, and then he started to make demands on Czechoslovakia for the return of the Sudeten Land, an area on the western side of that country which was the home for people who were mostly of German origin. All these were reported daily in the papers and on the news at the cinema and on the wireless. The events reported were always followed by discussions between the boys of Don's year and in particular with his close friend who introduced him to two young men, two or three years older than Don, who had just come back from fighting for the government in Madrid. It was not long before Don and his friends were singing one of the songs of the International Brigade, *No Pasarán* – They shall not Pass! He sang the song to his mum and dad – "Twenty years on into history has passed. Since red revolt was first victorious..." etc. and got a rebuke from his father, who, although a strong trade union man, did not like Communists.

Don and a small gang of friends met most evenings and at weekends in the Spot Snooker Club over Burtons in Enfield Town. He, not being at work, mostly watched the others playing snooker or table tennis as his pocket money did not stretch to paying for a table, but of course often he would be given a game by one of his friends. It was not usual for them to stay in the club long but it was a good meeting place to decide what they would be doing later that evening. Depending on the weather and how light the evenings were they would either go down to the park and play with a ball, or go to the pictures, or just walk up and down the town. Another meeting place was the busmen's café near the trolleybus terminal where the usual order was a cheesecake and a cup of tea for tuppence. Don was not too keen on cheesecake but there was really nothing else, so he did as the others. Another pastime on Saturdays was heckling at the street corner meetings of various speakers who invariably were either communist or fascist. At this time such meetings could be found in all the local boroughs and no doubt this was repeated all over the country. Young people were more politically minded then than at any time in Don's life. The meetings in Enfield were by the Town station, and in Edmonton, which was just up the road, they were held on The Green, which during the day was a market for stalls. The interest in politics by the young was probably more marked at this time as the issues of the day could be seen by most as likely to have a dramatic effect on their lives.

Chapter Six

It was during the summer holidays and a year after he had started at the new school that things really hotted up on the continent. Hitler's demands got louder and Chamberlain, the then Prime Minister of Britain, went to Germany to meet him and famously came back clutching a piece of paper that he said Hitler had signed which said that after the Sudetenland claim was settled he would have no other claims to make. Thus Britain agreed to him taking a part of Czechoslovakia in order to keep the peace. This became known as the Munich Crisis.

Don remembered it well as he had gone to London with his parents. His dad was taking his week's annual holiday and they were going to the theatre, to see, his parents had said, *The White Horse Inn*. Anyway they got to the theatre and the only tickets available were more money than his dad could afford so they looked around for somewhere else to go. All the time they were out Don had the German problem in the back of his mind; the morning headlines had been ominous to say the least. The only place they could get in was to see a play called *Thou Shall Not*, by, he believed, Emile Zola. It was at Wyndhams theatre and was quite unsuitable for him. Nevertheless, it was something that stuck in his mind and he would always associate it with the Munich Crisis.

The holidays came to an end and back at school the Headmaster called for a Thanksgiving Service now that the Prime Minister had recently said, "Peace in our time." However, Don and his friends having talked among themselves decided to boycott the service, as they did not believe there would be peace. The action of course did not go down well with the masters. Those who had boycotted the service were told to report to the Head, who interviewed each boy separately. Each of them simply said they did not believe war had been averted and that was it. The feeling was that the Head agreed with this too but had probably been obliged to hold the service through some directive from above.

Shortly after the thanksgiving episode the headmaster asked for volunteers from the sixth form to work in the evenings for a time to assemble gas masks. It was obvious that at long last those in power had really recognised that war was a strong possibility in the future and were beginning to prepare the nation. Don remembered reading in other people's papers whilst travelling to school in 1937 the arguments about disarmament, a policy Britain had adopted earlier much to the disgust of one politician, Winston Churchill, who had been labelled a warmonger. Don of course volunteered and cycled down to The Queensway in Ponders End, a part of Enfield close to the River Lea, where many factories had been built. The volunteers were soon instructed on what to do and for a few hours they assembled gas masks by joining the canister to the face piece by means of a strong rubber band and then packing the mask in a cardboard box. The work went on for just over two weeks when it seemed that factory's allocation for manufacture had been met and the masks were then ready for distribution throughout the country.

It was nevertheless a happy time for him at school but always in the background was the threat of war. Having finished with examinations he entered the sixth form, intending to stay at school until he found a job. He chose to go in the sixth commercial to study economics, commercial French and Spanish, plus learning typing and shorthand, all subjects which were designed to help in the outside world. The boys, who often seemed to be more interested in spending their time in the typing room learning to dance, treated none of the subjects very seriously as they were all simply there waiting for a job. Yes, dancing in the thirties was important for a young man who wanted to meet girls and so the boys acquired a book by Victor Sylvester on ballroom dancing and spent time between waiting for a turn on the typewriter following the steps marked in diagrams in the book. They learnt the quickstep, foxtrot, waltz and tango. Then there were races to see who could type, 'Now is the time for every young man to come to the aid of the party', fastest.

In between the school activities there was the serious side of writing for jobs. Don wrote to all the well-known high street banks, to all the insurance companies and many other firms who he knew had offices, but not once was he asked to come for an interview. He had been given excellent references from masters but they made no difference. The unemployment situation was grim and although times were better than earlier in the decade it was obvious that too many people were chasing too few jobs. His best friend Bob did get a job in the Westminster Bank, which Don was sure had come about because his father had a bank account. Don was pleased that Bob had got a job but it worried him that his parents still had to keep him at school. Of course Don's dad, as an engine driver, had no bank account. In fact very few manual workers had bank accounts at that time, and it did seem, as he had been told, it is not what you know that mattered but who you know.

Chapter Seven

Nevertheless, in spite of not getting anywhere with job seeking Don was happy at school and if he were honest with himself he did not really want it to end. He had only been at the school for a few months over a year and all accepted him as if he had been there all through the five years other pupils of his age had been at the school. Life was undoubtedly good. Things had happened to him that in his wildest dreams he had never expected when he had been forced to leave his old home, which now seemed as in another world. He was even invited out with others to dine with the headmaster; this was for all the boys in the school first eleven who had proved to be the best school team in the county. It was a first for Don; he had never been to a proper dinner before.

Don's sister, who was three years older than him, had got herself a job in Woolworths soon after they had moved to Enfield and one evening she came home to say all the girls were going on an outing to a London theatre and she asked Don if he would like to go. He happily accepted the offer and a few nights later he went with all the girls on a coach to the London Palladium to see *The Crazy Gang*. He enjoyed being with all the girls, the only young male present, and enjoyed the show too.

Then, shortly after, his parents took him to Glasgow to see the Empire Exhibition. It cost them not much more than the entrance fee because the fare was free; his dad using one of the three free passes issued to him each year by his employer for use on his railway, the London and North Eastern Railway (LNER). They travelled and slept overnight on the train in both directions in ordinary third-class compartments whilst spending the day at the exhibition. Yes, indeed life was good and yet there was always that strange feeling in the back of one's mind that it could not always be thus as war clouds were definitely gathering. Don remembered the stories of his dad in the World War of 1914–18 and although not mentioning to anyone his thoughts he wondered whether he would be lucky enough to survive if another war came about.

Then early one day he was told by his parents that they had spoken to the rent collector, whose mother owned the house in which they lived, about Don not being able to find a job and the man had said he knew someone who worked for the Metropolitan Water Board and would see if he could get an interview for him.

A few weeks later Don was sent a form to complete and in a covering letter was asked to forward his references for a possible interview at the Water Board. A few more weeks went by and finally he was called for the interview. He put on his best, in fact his only suit, and prepared to go up to London for his first interview for a job. The interview was to be in a building called New River Head which, he was told, was not far from The Angel, Islington. He could never remember being near there before but he recalled this was where John Gilpin had started his famous ride in the poem by William Cowper he had learnt at school. He could not help repeating to himself the first lines, "John Gilpin was a citizen of credit and renown, a train-band captain eke was he of famous London town" and remembered that Gilpin was supposed to stop at the Bell at Edmonton but rode through, no doubt going past somewhere near where Don now lived. How different the transport was then from now, he pondered. Don going in the reverse direction would have to catch a train to Stoke Newington and then get a bus for the remainder of the journey and he guessed it would take just as long as John Gilpin's ride, although probably more comfortable.

He set off to be in good time, got off the train at Stoke Newington and caught a bus to The Angel at Islington. He then walked down from the bus stop, passing the Sadlers Wells opera house, from which came the sound of singing, and so to the imposing building where he would have his interview. He was about fifteen minutes early so he walked on past the building, returning nearer to the time. He went in and was directed to an office on the ground floor where he was introduced to a gentleman sitting behind a big desk.

"You know Joe Salter, I understand?" he said.

"No, Sir, not exactly. You see my parents spoke to a man who owns the house we live in and he said he would ask his friend to try and get me an interview."

"I'll introduce you to Joe when we have finished, if you would like."

"Thank you, Sir, I would like to thank him, even if I am unsuccessful."

"Please sit down."

Don rather nervously sat in the chair facing the man. He had no idea what he would be asked, he had never asked any of his friends what they were asked when they went for their interviews.

"I have seen your references, they are very good. I see you were house captain and school football captain. Is it a big school?"

"About 600 boys I believe."

"I am now going to ask you a few questions, try not to worry they will not test your brain but just try to see what you know."

The interviewer then proceeded to ask questions like who is Prime Minister, what is the county town of Essex and which is the largest city in the world? These were easy meat to Don who for some years had studied the twelve encyclopaedias bought for him via *The Daily Herald* by his parents. He answered without any hesitation.

"Neville Chamberlain, Chelmsford and London."

"That's good; now can you give me the dates of Queen Victoria's reign?"

"1837 to 1901," Don quickly replied and the interviewer, who he learnt later was a Mr Coates, went on to explain a little about the company for whom he worked. He said the building they were in was built at the end of the New River, a river Don knew well as it ran through Enfield. The interviewer continued, "You know the river is entirely man-made, being built by Hugh Myddleton in the 1600s and was the first to bring fresh and clean water into London." He went on to explain how water rates were collected and who controlled the business, which he said was non-profit making. Having given Don a few more facts the meeting drew to a close.

"That is fine, I will be in touch. I have first to speak to the Revenue Officer who is responsible for this department." He paused, "Shall we go and meet Joe Salter?"

They duly found his benefactor and Don thanked him.

Ten minutes later Don was walking back to where he would catch his bus. He felt different, it was a strange feeling and he knew within that his life was about to change; he would soon be a working man. As he made his way home almost in a trance, his mind wandered over the events of the past hour and he hardly noticed he had boarded a bus. It was some time later, when the bus was well on its way that he came to and began to take notice of things around. Although he knew he had not yet got the job, he could see the change in his life would not be too far off. He returned to Enfield and back to school.

Chapter Eight

Starting Work

A few weeks went by and finally he got a letter that said he could start work at New River Head on the date shown but first he must complete, sign and return the form enclosed. He straightway showed his parents and then sat back and contemplated how now his life would change. He had only three more weeks at school and would then start his first job. No it wasn't his first job, after all he did do that milk round for a few weeks and then there was the butcher's round. Don smiled to himself as he remembered the two previous small jobs. They were only a little time ago and yet already had passed into the background so that he had almost forgotten it was in fact work.

First there came the milk round. He remembered that it was his mother who had got him that job when one day near Christmas the milkman, arriving late, told her that he could not push the barrow as the snow was so deep. "My son will help if you like," she had said and within a few minutes Don had put on some warm clothes and was out pushing the barrow and helping deliver milk. Back at the depot, which was over the nearby railway bridge close by his home, the milkman asked Don if he would like to come and help while the snow was about. Don of course agreed and the next morning he was over at the depot before five o'clock and loading the barrow for the first round. In those days the milkman did two deliveries each day, the first very early morning when milk was put on the doorsteps and the second was to take extra orders for milk and butter etc. and to collect the money. The snow that winter was very deep and stayed for a long time and so did Don. He smiled as he remembered the milkman's orders, "Give no. 12 two and drop one over at 14." Drop one over, he smiled, it is a wonder I didn't do just that, he thought, my hands were frozen. But of course there was that nice hot cup of tea he was given when he got back to the depot, he was sure tea had never tasted so good. How much the milkman gave him for his help he could not quite remember but of course it would be nothing like the money he would soon be earning in his new job, twenty-seven shillings and sixpence each week!

The second job he had was around another Christmas and only lasted a week or so, but it was memorable. It came about when his namesake 'cousin', known to the Moggs household as Little Don, said the butcher he worked for at the weekends wanted some more help over the Christmas period and wondered if Don would like to earn some money. He had jumped at the opportunity and being on holiday had gone straightway with Little Don on their bikes to the nearby Palmers Green. He was introduced to the butcher and then to the bike he would have to ride. It had a big basket over a small wheel in the front with a normal wheel and seat behind. Now Palmers Green and the nearby Winchmore Hill were posh areas to young Don, not so many terraced houses as in Enfield, and the people who lived there he would later come to know as being middle class, but at the time they were just posh; this was before he had moved to his own posh road when his grandfather came to live with them. Soon after he arrived he had been given a quantity of meat properly labelled that he had to load in the basket and then, armed with a list of calls to be made, set off on his first delivery. The butcher and Little Don had told him roughly where the roads were but he did not have the benefit of a map and thus this first foray included many rides up and down roads more than once, but he soon became familiar with the roads in the area. Nearer Christmas day the meat to be delivered was of course mostly turkey and although he did not lose any birds from the basket it was a near thing. Most of the area covered was hilly and the best part of trips out for him was when he was able to race down the many hills without applying the brakes causing the meat and turkeys to bounce dangerously up and down until the incline on the other side slowed him and forced him to dismount and push the heavy bike and meat up the other side. One day he met a lad from his class at school, the boy living locally, and Don was mildly embarrassed that the word might get around at school that he, House Captain, Football Captain and Prefect, was also a butcher's boy! But it never did, or if it did no one bothered or were too frightened of him to say anything.

Yes, he mused, he had worked a little but that would be nothing compared to what he would shortly be doing.

His last few weeks at school were quite uneventful and apart from saying farewell to the few classmates of the Sixth Commercial and to one or two teachers whom he happened to see on his last day, nothing much happened. It was of course not the end of term when there would have been considerable handshaking and general jollity, instead the leaving was hardly noticed and indeed to Don was a big anticlimax.

On the Monday morning he was due to start work he got up early, having the previous night worked out which train he would catch and pressed his fifty shilling suit that he left hanging on the picture rail in the front room where there had been a good fire in the grate that evening. He walked over to the railway station nearby and purchased a return ticket to Stoke Newington. The station platform was quite crowded but when the train came in he was able to get a corner seat in a non-smoking compartment. At Stoke Newington he got out and left the station, intending to catch a bus to The Angel at Islington. He had looked up at the station clock as he left the platform and realised he had an hour before he was due to start work and if he caught a bus right away he would be at work much too early. He decided he would start to walk and catch the bus further along the route. Although he had only been along this route once before he thought he would soon recognise the road and in any case buses would pass him and very soon he would join the tramlines which would go all the way to The Angel. Half an hour later he realised he was on the final stretch of road that would lead to where he would have got off the bus and it would not now be worth bothering to ride as it was only a five minute walk from the bus stop to his final destination, New River Head. It was quite a dull day but he had nevertheless enjoyed the walk and had saved his bus fare. He was soon passing the Sadlers Wells theatre, but this time too early to expect the sound of singing or music to come through the open doors it now being only the abode of cleaners finishing off their morning stint, and then a short way along he was at the foot of the impressive steps which led to the many doors into New River Head. He hesitated before climbing the steps and was joined by a young man wearing a smart suit, pinstripe trousers and black jacket, and carrying a rolled umbrella. "You look as if you are starting today?" the young man said, "I am too, my name is Jeremy Mabbutt," he held out his hand.

Don took his hand, "Does it look that obvious? Yes, you are right, I'm Don – shall we go in?"

The two young men entered the building and asked a messenger near the door the way to the office where they had been told to report. They were both shown to the room and then after signing a book were taken along a corridor and into what they were told was The Revenue Hall where they would both be given their first task. The hall was filled with a number of rows of high desks stretching from one side of the hall to the other and every few feet people were sitting on high stools on both sides of the desks along the centre of which were brass rails in which were placed wicker baskets. Don was taken to one of the desks and introduced to those people immediately close by and opposite to where he was told would be his position. One young man was told to explain to him what he would be doing for the next few days.

"I'm Ted Moon, I've been working here a couple of years. The job you will do first we call marrying." Ted produced two huge piles of what Don could see were notices of some sort; one had black print and the other red. "These are, as you can guess, water rate notices and your job will be to make one pile by putting the red notice behind the black, in other words, marry them. The completed piles are then given for distribution to the various offices whose staff will insert carbon paper, write the notices and send out the top copy, keeping the red for sending out if payment is not made on the first notice." Don said he understood and climbing up on his stool started marrying! He was told his lunch break would be at one o'clock and would last one hour.

At one o'clock Ted took him upstairs and showed him the dining room where he could eat. "The meals, I am told, are very cheap but I bring my own." Don said he would do the same. It was then he realised that he had quite forgotten to bring any food, but he did not let on to Ted, instead thanked him and said he would see him later. He looked at his five shilling watch on his wrist, given to him by his parents, and checked it with the clock in the Revenue Hall – he had forty-five minutes before he was due back at his desk and in that time he would go out of the building and walk around the streets. The only money he had was his bus fare back to Stoke Newington boosted by his walking in from there in the morning, hardly enough to buy anything much to eat. He retraced his steps towards The Angel stopping outside Sadlers Wells and listening to the singing coming from within, then further up the road he entered a sweet shop and bought himself a tuppenny bar of Cadbury's chocolate with his morning bus fare. He continued walking up to City Road and returned via the back streets he judged would take him to the office.

The afternoon soon passed and at the appointed hour a bell rang and everyone started to leave. He learnt Ted was going over to London Bridge to catch a train to Catford and Ted had told him the others he had been introduced to would be going to a variety of places – some by tram to Waterloo to catch trains going out to Surrey, others going on the underground to places in east and west London, whilst others were walking to Kings Cross and St Pancras to go home to places in Hertfordshire and Bucks. None of those he knew would be going his way.

He had an uneventful journey home and while eating the hot meal his mother had prepared, he related all that had happened to him on that first day.

"My goodness, did you do that all day?" his sister asked.

"Yes all day, and I am told I will be doing it all week."

"A child could do that," she said. "Fancy all that trouble to get the job and then do that."

"I imagine I will do bigger things when I have been there a while."

"Did you have to make the tea?" she laughingly said.

"No, that was brought round to us. But we have to pay for it..." he hesitated, "at the end of the week of course – just as well as I only had my bus money with me."

"I did more important things than that when I started work and I was only fourteen and never had the benefit of a Grammar School education!" she added.

Don didn't know what to say, he knew it was true but it wasn't his fault. He always got on well with his sister but he knew she resented the fact that he had been kept on at school for so long after the age she had had to leave.

His sister at fourteen had had to travel by train up to London each day to work in a small shop owned by the Royal Worcester China Company, which he thought was in Holborn, and certainly had been given more responsible work than he had been given. Among the jobs she was given was to take expensive china pieces to various London hotels, such as the Savoy and Dorchester. She said she never went round to the back of the hotel to deliver but marched in through the front entrance, mind you no one seeing this attractive young lady would have guessed she was only fourteen. Yes she did do more than him.

Chapter Nine

The remainder of the week at work passed much as he had been told it would – he was 'marrying' all the time. On Friday he was paid, it was the most money he had ever had – twenty-seven shillings and sixpence! When he got home he handed fifteen shillings over to his mother and asked if it was enough. She said it was plenty and hoped he had enough for himself.

"You'll need it as you will have to start buying your own clothes now and of course you have got your fares!"

"I'll manage, Mum," Don said, and he knew he would as twelve and sixpence was much more than he had ever had.

That evening he went out and met the boys in The Spot Club over Montague Burtons in Enfield Town. As has been said before this was a favourite place for the young men where one could spend time playing snooker or table tennis while making up your mind what big adventure to undertake later in the evening. Of course he now had enough money to pay for a game of snooker or table tennis himself instead of just watching or occasionally getting a game with one of the working lads with money. That evening it was decided they would go to the pictures and so they went along to the ABC cinema where they knew one got a good evening's entertainment. They would get the usual two good films, the newsreel, a cartoon, an organ interlude, and a half-hour stage show. Four hours of entertainment for sixpence, or if those seats were filled, since it was later in the evening, one shilling!

The following week at work he was asked if he wanted to play football for the Water Board, it seems the news had got around that he played. He was told he could have a game in the fourth team to start with and someone would be there to judge how he played. The game would be at home on the following

Saturday. It seemed the Water Board ran four teams all called Aquarius; the first team was in the Southern Amateur league and the second in the Nemean League, all high up in the amateur game. The home ground was at Honor Oak, "Where's that?" Don asked. "It's in Surrey," the football representative answered. In those days anywhere south of the river in the London area was Surrey, hence Surrey County Cricket being at the Oval, which nowadays is a long way from the Surrey county boundary.

Don had only ever been south of the river in London once before and that was when he was very young and went with his parents to visit an aunt who lived there. South of the river was another world to those who came from the north side, for one thing the place was full of trams whereas apart from the tram which ran south from the Manor House and along past Don's work, all trams on the north side had long since been taken off and trolleybuses put in their place. Then instead of steam trains, as there were in the north, all the suburban railways above ground south of the river were electric and it was on one of these trains that Don made his first journey to Honor Oak.

Most of the men in the fourth eleven were much older than Don and had obviously been playing with each other for some time. They clearly enjoyed their football but had no aspirations to play for one of the better teams. Aquarius lost the game by the odd goal but Don must have impressed someone watching because on the Monday he was asked if he would like to play for the second eleven who had a game away from home against Winchmore Hill. He readily agreed particularly as he lived very near to the ground on which the game would be played.

At the office work continued as hitherto, but at the end of the third week it ended and he was introduced to a ledger that listed all properties against which were shown the rateable values and amounts due. He was then shown how when someone paid their rate this amount was posted, a new meaning of the word for Don, to the ledger by writing through a carbon strip, this slip being used for balancing the day's takings. This posting was generally done in pencil as using ink was a slower process, since putting extra pressure on a pen so as to get a distinct copy in the ledger invariably meant spreading the nib and in any event ink had to be dried. Ballpoint pens had not been introduced in the thirties.

Having been given some idea of how to operate a ledger and given a task to perform, he happily started his fourth week in the Revenue Hall. However, on Tuesday he was informed that he would be moving away from Head Office and should report to a new office that was opening in Tottenham the following day. He had just got to know the ladies and men working around him and was a little sorry to have to leave but of course the new office would be much nearer home and he would be able to save on fares as he was sure he would be able to ride his bicycle to work. He said his farewells to Ted and his new-found friends and left for home that evening armed with the address of the new office.

The following morning he set off early on his bicycle for Tottenham. For those who do not know, Tottenham was then a London borough, although in more recent years it has been amalgamated with another borough, and the name was known throughout the country because of its football team, Tottenham Hotspur, known as the Spurs, then the richest club in the country. Don had been taken there not long ago by his uncle and also to a few games by his dad and like him had from a small boy looked upon it as his team. After riding for some fifteen minutes he passed the ground at White Hart Lane, and continued along the High Road until he reached the numbers that indicated he was close to his destination. He found the office up a short drive; on one side was Barclays Bank and on the other an Italian workman's café. He was the first to arrive and the door into the office was locked. Although it was early in March it was quite a warm day and the sun was shining. He leant his bicycle against the wall and waited. Some ten minutes later a lady and gentleman arrived, Charlie Moore and Mrs Biggs. The former, Don learnt later, would be the under boss and had a key to the office. He told Don to bring his bike inside and lean it against the wall in the entrance lobby. Double swing doors led to the public's front office where there was a solid looking counter plus a desk and chair near one of the big windows overlooking the drive. Through another door was the main office with a big desk in the middle of the room, one similar to those he had got used to in the Revenue hall, and it had four stools around it. Three low desks completed the furniture in the office. There was also a big open fireplace that was meant to heat this main office while sending some heat to the others where additional heat was given by an electric fire – there was no central heating. Next to arrive was the boss, a Mr Haynes, who became known as Horace, he had a separate office whilst the under boss had his desk in the main office near to the fire. Two other men arrived together soon after. One in his mid-twenties lived locally and became known as Smithy whilst the other a little younger lived a short trolleybus ride nearer London and near to the Arsenal football ground that he naturally supported. The latter was called George, although this was not his first name, he said if you ever come to my house don't ask for George as all the men were known with this name; his surname was Washington. The last to arrive was Don Varnier, a small man with a deep voice, who was to sit out in the front office and would be available to answer any awkward questions raised by the public; he was third in seniority, a man in his early forties.

Don was told the office would not be opening for business until the following Monday and the task this week would be to get everything ready for the opening. The first job he was given was to make the tea, the usual job for the junior. He then had to light the fire, which had been made ready by those who had prepared the office for the new arrivals; the coal he found was kept in a bunker outside, near the back door. The office, a single-storey building next to an old brewery, was directly below a railway embankment that curved into the nearby railway station of Bruce Grove. The building had been erected as an office for use by the brewery but it became surplus to their requirements and so now was rented out to the Water Board. In accordance with most commercial premises the brewery had the previous year, at the time of the 'Munich Crisis', built a small air raid shelter behind the building and above ground.

Don walked round to examine the shelter to compare it with the one he had helped his father build in the garden at home. That was the time when the government had issued air-raid shelters to all households; those for people who had a garden were called Anderson shelters and were made of heavy corrugated iron. He and his dad had sunk theirs about two feet in the garden and the earth taken from the hole was then thrown on top giving, it was hoped, further protection for those inside. He hoped they would never have to use it, but he had his doubts.

Over the next two or three days, work in the office was allocated – those senior to him being given 'districts' that would be their responsibility to control as far as payment of rates were concerned. Tottenham had at that time a population of about 160,000 but since the collection area allocated to the new office overlapped adjoining boroughs Don learnt the seven staff of the office would be responsible for close on 200,000 people. All of this he told his parents. At least now he believed he had a job, even though he would only be looking after mundane matters in the office.

Chapter Ten

One of the jobs he was given was to keep a record of postage stamps and embossed envelopes, the latter being used to send out the notices to customers. The envelopes were embossed with green halfpenny stamps and were in boxes of 500 each. In the stamp book he was meant to enter every stamp used. However, before the week was out he was told by Charlie Moore that he had better put a few extra names in the book each day as staff frequently raided the stamps, either sending out mail that Don did not see or taking stamps for personal use. At the end of each day it was also his job to collect the outgoing post, enter it in the book and then take it over the road to the post office. Don did as he was told and naively assumed the entering of extra names was what every post boy was expected to do, he had never heard of an internal audit section and was surprised one day when someone came into the office and asked to see his stamp book and stamps. Don asked him if he wanted to see his reserves and was surprised to learn that this man was not pleased to know that this was the way he controlled the use of stamps. He was called into the boss and was told he must not keep reserves – Don explained that sometimes mail went out without him seeing it and that there would be a discrepancy if he did not do something to counter this. The explanation was only partly accepted and the boss had to issue instructions that the person entering the stamp book must see all mail going out. Of course Horace knew the score but had to pretend he did not and so Don got the blame but was excused as a new boy. It was a pity someone had not told me about Internal Audit, he thought!

By the end of March he had really settled in to his work at the small office in Tottenham and actually enjoyed being there.

Each day was different and he got on well with all the staff and they seemed to like him too. He particularly enjoyed going out on odd jobs for them, buying firelighters, ordering some coal, or buying a bar of chocolate, knowing whoever had asked him to get it would give him a square for himself. Yes life was good and much better being there than in the Revenue Hall in town.

One evening he went along with his friends to a dance and having learnt some of the dance steps from the Victor Sylvester book whilst at school, plucked up courage to ask a young lady for a dance. After one or two dances he soon found he could manage the waltz and quickstep without crushing his partner's toes and then later after visiting more dances and with further schooling from his sister, a very good dancer who had already won a number of dance competitions, he was soon managing the foxtrot, the hardest of the basic ballroom dances to perform properly. However, up until then he had never taken a girl out on a date, in fact he had hardly spoken to any except those at work in London and of course the girls he had asked for a dance. He began to wonder how he appeared to the opposite sex, his sister had said he was good looking but he reasoned she might just be saying that. But he did remember one incident whilst at school which meant that at least some girls had taken an interest in him. It happened when he was first playing football at the new school when some girls from the nearby school had appeared over the fence dividing their school from his school's playing fields. Then with a twinkle in his eye one of the team had told him that they were asking who this new boy was.

Of course he wanted to know girls but was, he guessed, a little shy about speaking to them without being introduced. Now of course the dances would give him his opportunity. There was one girl who used to hang around with one or two of his friends whom he was particularly fond of but he had no confidence about asking her on a date although he did try to meet her as if by chance. He found out where she worked and at what time she left the factory. So sometimes, if he got off work in good time, he would cycle hard to the factory before going home in the hope that he would bump into her. But on the first few occasions his courage faltered and instead of riding alongside her as she rode her bicycle from the factory he simply looked and then rode home. He was obviously smitten but had yet to speak to her. Even his young cousin Harry, with whom he was in the habit of going for a walk on most Sunday mornings, knew he liked the girl as he found their Sunday morning walk began to take them past the girl's house, although they never once saw her.

He eventually plucked up courage on one visit to the factory gates and casually rode up to her and all her friends and engaged her in conversation. By the time they got near to her home he had asked her if she would like to come out with him one evening and she agreed. He took her to the pictures, paying for the expensive seats at the back of the cinema. But that was that, he never asked her out again although he often wondered why and whether she wondered why too! She eventually married a boy from Don's school, but that is another story.

There were dances held at many halls around his area, some regular and others held for special occasions, but it was easy to find a dance most nights of the week. Don and his friends now started frequenting the local dance halls and some went for lessons at a hall in Winchmore Hill where the teacher, as they said 'an old man', insisted his pupils learnt not only the then accepted basic ballroom dances but also the Lancers which he so obviously enjoyed. It was customary if you liked a girl to try and get the last dance with her and then perhaps ask to see her home. The last dance was always a waltz when the lights in the hall would invariably be dimmed. One night Don managed to get the last waltz with a good-looking girl he had danced with once before that evening. Her name was Millie, which later tickled his friends, and he asked to see her home but she said she was going home with some other girls but that she would like to see him again, so he made a date to meet her outside one of the cinemas. She was there waiting for him when he arrived for the date two nights later. Oh no, Don wasn't late, he was always on time or early, just like his dad who was always in trouble from his wife because he always got her to the station to catch a train long before the train was due and she had to sit there, sometimes in the cold, just because he could not bear being late.

Anyway, cinemas in those days had continuous programmes and unless you made sure you went in at the beginning of a film or perhaps when the organ was playing, the chances are you would arrive in the middle of a film and then you would stay until that part came round again, hence the expression, "that's where we came in". After they reached the part where they came in, Don and his girlfriend left. Don learnt that she lived a good way from the cinema and although it was light, being high summer, he offered to take her home, he wanted to talk to her anyway. They had to catch a bus and then change to a trolleybus and when they eventually arrived she said, "I live down the road opposite the bus stop," and Don noticed she appeared to hesitate about him walking along with her. Anyway, they crossed the road and started down the road opposite. They did not walk fast and he noticed that however slow he walked two big men seemed to follow at the same distance behind. He wondered whether they were going to try and jump him and inwardly he prepared himself for a fight but said nothing to the girl. Soon she stopped and said this was her house. As they stopped by the gate Don noticed the two men had stopped too and started talking to each other. "Have you noticed the two men following us?" he asked. "Oh yes, it's all right, they're my brothers." Don didn't stay long talking but said he had to go, shook hands with the young lady and left. He never saw her again but had a laugh over it when he saw his friends. "I reckon she's still at school!" one of them said.

That season Don continued to play a few games for the Aquarius second eleven, the team having mixed results. Then one day his under boss came to tell him a call had come through from Head Office asking whether he could play the next day for the first team in the Southern Amateur League. They had to know right away. He of course said he would and was surprised when the boss came from his office to congratulate him on being picked. It was, however, the last game of the season and although unaware of it at the time it was to be the last game he played for Aquarius. He had a good game, although unlike most games he had played in over the past few years, he did not score.

Easter came around and his friends had decided to go to the Daily Worker camp being held outside a small village in Hertfordshire. They asked him to come along with them. He had not joined the YCL (Young Communist League) as had most of those he would be going with; in fact one, Ron, was the local secretary. Anyway his parents did not object to him going although they told him not to join the YCL; he told them he had no intention of joining but was just going along for, as his friends had said, a fun weekend.

So on Good Friday they caught the train from Enfield Chase Farm station and on to Bayford, a few stops down the line. The camp was in a big field close by, with tents already erected. Jim and Adam, the two lads who had not long been back from fighting in Madrid, joined them and Don listened intently to the stories these two told them, and joined in the singing which inevitably followed. The weekend was most successful but Don, quite unused to sitting in the sun, got pretty burnt around the face in the unseasonably hot weather.

Chapter Eleven

Soon after Easter a fair arrived in Bush Hill Park and one evening he went along with his friend Del and two girls who had attached themselves to the gang. It was dusk when they left the bright lights of the fair and walking slowly along talking they accidentally bumped into some people going in to the fair. One of the two who they had bumped into let out some abusive language that Don did not like and being in the company of two young ladies he went back and reprimanded the person. The man who had sworn was about the size of Don. Words were exchanged and the other man suddenly said, "If it's a fight you want you've got it." Del came up and said, "I'll fight him for you." Don said, "No, Del, it's my fight," and started to take off his jacket. Del said afterwards he took one look at the big man who had been half hidden in the dusk light and decided to let Don have the fight. Now Don had done a lot of boxing, in fact for four years he had at his previous school boxed regularly and had only been beaten once; he knew he was no pushover. However, street fighting, he was soon to learn, was not quite the same as the Marquis of Queensbury rules and having landed a couple of straight lefts on the man's face the next thing he knew was that his head was under the man's arm and his face was being pummelled so that blood spurted from his nose and he went down to the ground. By this time a crowd had gathered and remarks were being made about picking on a young lad and Don realised he had been knocked out for a second or two. Del was peering over him and getting him to his feet, the two men were walking off and the smaller of the two called out, "That will teach you to pick a fight with a real boxer."

The crowd began to disperse with one man saying, "Are you all right, son, do you want me to call the police?" Don assured him he was OK and that he did not want the police. Del said he would take him to his home nearby and clean him up. Del's house was near the park gates and Don was soon looking more respectable and his friend said he would walk home with him. When they got near to Don's house Del could see there was a light and, knowing Don's father, decided he would leave Don to face the music alone. He went in and sure enough his dad was still up and looking at his son said, "What's all this, been in a fight at one of these communist meetings you keep going to? I told you to keep away." Don explained what had happened.

The following morning he decided to go to work by train as it was pouring with rain, but being very conscious of the state of his face, his nose in particular, he bought a paper, which he had never done before, and sat in a corner seat holding the paper in front of his face. At work he had his leg pulled a lot by the fellows but had a good deal of sympathy from Mrs Biggs.

The next night while walking with some of his friends in Enfield Town centre, several girls came up to him and asked if he was all right. It seems the news of the fight had got around and although he had lost he had become a bit of a hero for being prepared to fight.

His friend Bob, who most of the gang respected and who in later years he thought was a Marlon Brando lookalike, decided they should look for the man and as he put it, "sort him out". They looked around the park area, the fair had gone that morning, and in the town area but never found the man who Del said he would recognise, although Don laughingly said, "I doubt whether I would know him, I hardly saw his face." Perhaps to save the face of the gang it was decided that the man was almost certainly from the boxing booth as surely no one could otherwise have made such a mess of their man.

Chapter Twelve

The summer months of 1939 slowly passed and Don was happy in his work. Although there was a lot to do they all worked well together, seeming to enjoy each other's company and having many good laughs. Don had told the others that his dad, an engine driver, drove trains on the line which went past the back of the office and after he had once waved to his dad, it became routine for staff in the office to wave at the engine when they recognised the driver leaning and waving from the cab, on the up line to the Liverpool Street terminus, as the train was slowing to enter the nearby station.

During the summer months staff took their holidays, most going away to various places in England as was usual in those days. But Don had no holiday, as he would not be entitled to any annual leave until he had completed one year. It did not bother him as he enjoyed going to work and in any case knew he would be entitled to one week next year. They worked every day except Sundays, although only a half-day on Saturdays, and he was entitled to have five of these off each year; others got more for longer service. He became quite friendly with Mrs Biggs, who took a motherly interest in him, and one day she said her daughter was having a party and asked if he would like to come. He wasn't keen on going but did not like to refuse. The mother and daughter lived alone, he never did find out what had happened to the father, all he knew was that Charlie Moore, the under boss, and Mrs Biggs were pretty good friends and always came to the office together. He found the daughter was a nice young girl but not someone he wanted to get involved with although her mother was obviously keen to make a match and arranged for Don to take the girl one evening to a dance near her home.

Don was only seventeen and at an age when he was trying to be very adult. In those days he knew the man was always expected to pay when taking a lady out and although the young lady did not offer to pay for herself she caused him some embarrassment when having been asked if she would like some refreshments, she asked those serving at the refreshment counter the price of each item before choosing what she would have. It was obvious her mother had told her that he did not earn much and so she should make sure not to allow him to spend much, a very kind thought but something Don did not enjoy happening when trying to be grown up. He never asked the girl out again.

One evening his dad announced that they would be going to a shop in Enfield Town to see television. The BBC had started the first television broadcasts from Alexandra Palace, about four miles distance, a couple of years before but of course only those people with a lot of money could afford to buy a set to pick up the programmes being offered. Don and his family never knew or heard of anyone having a set, indeed had never seen one. There were no shops in Enfield having sets to sell until this brand new shop announced it would be demonstrating television. His dad had managed to get tickets for the show and thus seated with four or five other people in a small room over the shop, those present saw television for the first time. The set had a small nine-inch screen and they were shown a film, *The Drum*, with a new young Indian as the star, Sabu. They were told that there would be little chance of getting a set for some time because with a war imminent manufacturers were turning to munitions etc, not that his parents could have afforded one anyway.

It was late summer when he received a letter asking him to come along for a trial for Enfield Football Club, telling him to bring a full kit and a white shirt. Enfield FC was then in the Athenian league one of the top amateur leagues in the country. The club had good support and pulled in good crowds, especially for the local derby with Barnet seven miles away. A couple of days later the local newspaper had details of the trial and a small write-up on the new boy. His dad was quite excited over it as he had for many years as a young man followed the local team both on their old ground, in Cherry Orchard Lane, and then in their new super stadium in Southbury Road. The trial was to take place on Wednesday, 23rd August, 1939.

Don duly went along to the stadium on the evening of the 23rd and played two halves in his usual position, inside left. He did not have a particularly good game but after the game and a hot shower, he was told to lie on a table for a massage. He had never had a massage before and it made him feel very important – this is something I could get quite used to, he thought. However, on the Sunday of the following week things all changed – all sport, cinemas, theatres and other places of entertainment were closed as war had been declared on Germany.

That Sunday was 3rd September and on such a day, as the weather was fair, Don's cousin Harry duly arrived for their morning walk. However, because there was going to be an important broadcast on the wireless at eleven and it was now nearly half past ten they decided to wait to hear what was going to be said. The previous evening the British government had issued an ultimatum to Berlin to the effect that if Germany did not cease activities against Poland, a country they had invaded two days before, then a state of war would exist between Britain and Germany. At eleven Neville Chamberlain, the British Prime Minister, announced that as no reply had been received, Britain was now at war with Germany. What Don and his friends at school had always suspected would happen, had indeed come about. He of course was not pleased to be right as he knew in his mind that unless the war were over quickly he would likely be involved at some time.

After discussing the news with Harry and his parents the two boys decided they would go out on their walk anyway. They left the house and had walked no more than two hundred yards when the air raid sirens were sounded and they made a hasty retreat back home. Nothing happened and the 'all clear' siren soon sounded; it was assumed the raid must be somewhere else or it was just a practice to see how people reacted. The remainder of that day was quiet as were the next and the next, and thus began what later became known as the phoney war. A week or two later and still nothing untoward had happened on the home front so the government decided to allow cinemas and other places of entertainment to reopen. The football programmes, however, were all changed and to avoid travelling it was decided to rearrange all leagues; also many teams, aware that more men would be called to the colours, which had already started, and again so as to avoid unnecessary travel, decided to drop reserve sides. Don heard no more from Enfield and assumed their reserve side had ceased.

He read his dad's paper every day and listened to the wireless, always hoping there would be some dramatic move by the allied armies that would take the Germans by surprise and hasten the war's end, but nothing happened. It was a strange war, the British Expeditionary Force settled in France with the French stationed along the much-vaunted Maginot Line. The wireless from time to time reported one or two forays towards the Germans entrenched behind the Seigfried Line but nothing of significance happened. There was, however, action at sea and whilst German submarines were sinking vessels in the Atlantic, three small cruisers engaged the German pocket battleship *Graf Spee* in the South Atlantic and forced her into Montevideo harbour, from whence she scuttled herself.

In November the Russians invaded Finland but initially were given a bloody nose by the small but well-trained Finnish army. The Finns adapted better to the harsh winter conditions and the Russians suffered very heavy losses until the Spring came when a peace treaty was signed, Finland giving up a part of their territory. Russia was of course given bad press in England and anyone with communist connections was likely to be visited by Foreign Office officials. It was thus at this time that Don's friend Ron, secretary of the local Young Communist League, had a visit and had papers naming members taken. All of which was to change a few months later when Germany invaded Russia and that country then becoming an ally.

Chapter Thirteen

It was early in the war that Don's sister, Babs, as she liked to be known, met a sergeant in the army and soon married him. He lived in Derby and she went up there to live for a while. However, the marriage did not last and she later divorced him, but at that time Don was already away in the services. He understood later that she had managed the whole divorce on her own, not an easy matter in those days. Don did not know the grounds for the divorce but guessed it was infidelity.

The 'Call up' of men to the forces continued apace. The wireless and newspapers giving details of what ages were being called and when they should register. The first calls had been made soon after the Munich Crisis the previous year. Don was not yet eighteen and no date had at that time been given for when he would be due to register. He and his friends, a few months older than him, had decided they would go in the RAF to train as aircrew. Then towards the end of 1939 one of the gang of fellows he went around with had a nasty accident to his eye whilst at work and it became obvious that following this he would not be accepted in any of the services. It appears that someone in the factory where he worked shot something across the room, probably a paperclip, and hit Frank in the eye and blinded him.

At the office in Tottenham both George and Smithy registered and it was known they would soon be called up. George had opted for the Navy and Smithy for the RAF. Christmas came and went and still nothing much on the war front happened. Don and his friends still met regularly, played snooker, went to the pictures and did a round of the local dance halls where they soon became known and respected as persons no one messed with. The Aquarius teams not operating, Don got involved with old boys' football and was soon turning out regularly for the first eleven.

Spring brought some good weather and Don became due for his first holiday from work, one week for having completed a year's service. His friend Bob was also eligible for holiday from the Westminster Bank and the two of them decided to fix a holiday together. They agreed on a cycle holiday down to the West Country. Bob had a recent model racing bike whilst Don had the same bike his parents had given him when he was twelve, both bikes had dropped handle bars but of course no gears; the only bicycles with gears at that time, all only three speed, were usually ridden by old men, it being thought by the young to be sissy to have gears. Bob and Don had one week for the holiday and they left Enfield at lunchtime after finishing work on the Saturday morning; it was the 11th April, 1940. Don had been given a little book of atlases of the British Isles for getting distinction in Geography in the Matric and armed with this they set off for the West.

They cycled across London to the A30, the then main road to the West, and by late afternoon they came to the small town of Basingstoke. They decided to spend their first night here and soon found a cheap bed and breakfast. In the evening they managed to find a local hop (dance) and returned to the B&B just before eleven, the time they had been told the door would be shut.

The following morning at breakfast they sat with a soldier who was on a short leave. He told them he had just come back from the north of Norway where British troops had landed in the hope of forestalling a German takeover. Don and Bob listened intently and it made them realise that at last something was beginning to happen. They left Basingstoke straight after breakfast and continued down the A30. The weather for the time of the year was very good, the sun was shining and the countryside was beautiful. The roads were almost deserted, very few cars but quite a number of army vehicles including many low loaders carrying tanks. Cycling along at that time in the beautiful country was a lovely way of travelling, with the only noise coming from birds, the hum of tyres and, depending on speed, the whistling of wind in the ears. Soon they were crossing Salisbury Plain, an area that for years had been a training ground for the Army, and as they rode along convoys of lorries passed them from time to time, many loaded with troops. There was much waving by the soldiers as they passed the two cyclists and many cries of "they'll get you soon". This, and the meeting with the soldier, were the only times during their week away that they were reminded that there was a war on. They stopped by the roadside to eat the sandwiches the B&B lady had cut for them and then cycled on. At about five o'clock they entered Yeovil and again found a B&B. After a wash and brush-up they found a small workman's café and bought a meal, and took a walk around the town before returning to their lodgings. Don posted a card home on which he had written the story of their journey so far.

The following morning they headed further down the A30, through Honiton and towards Exeter. Neither of them had ever been to the West of England but with the aid of the small atlas and the plentiful signposts they were always sure where they were. Don had had many train journeys with his parents but had never been west of London with them because his father's railway, on which they had certain free travel, went only north and east of London. The railways covering the West Country at that time were the Great Western and the Southern Railway. Looking at the map they decided that it would be nice to find a place on the coast for the next night's stay over, and so they agreed to take the new bypass around Exeter in the hope of making the coast before nightfall. Don had brought with him a tiny box camera he had bought through the new magazine *Modern Wonder* and it was here that he took his first pictures on the journey. They followed the road that was signed Torquay and arrived there at about six in the evening. They rode along the front at Torquay but could not find a cheap B&B but continuing on through to Paignton they were successful in getting one for 2/6d each. There was plenty to see that evening and they eventually returned to the lodge at about ten o'clock. They asked the lady if they could have an early breakfast, as they wanted to get started early the next morning; she agreed and said she would call them at six.

They set off at seven on a road that would take them on to Dartmoor with the intention of riding north until they reached Lynton and Lynmouth, which they hoped to make by nightfall. However, they had not realised how hilly it was on the moor and they soon knew they would not get to their destination before dark. Cycling down hills on the moor was very exciting and they guessed speeds of up to sixty miles an hour were frequently reached, but nearly always on the other side they spent too much time walking as with no gears they could not force the bikes up many of the hills. Having been riding and walking for over six hours they were beginning to feel hungry but the moor on the road they travelled hardly had any villages and there was nothing where they could have eaten. Soon they came to a place marked on the map as Two Bridges and across from where they were riding there was an hotel. By this time they were desperately hungry and even though this did not look to be the sort of place they would normally enter they resolved to go in. The hotel was to them 'high class' and neither had been in such a place before and of course they were hardly attired for the hotel dining room, nor did they know whether they would have enough money for a meal, but nevertheless went in and sat down. There were a few other people sitting at tables and since the boys had not noticed any cars outside when they had come in they guessed these people must be guests in the hotel. Both of them had read in the papers recently that the government had fixed the maximum price that could be charged for a meal at five shillings but they wondered if the hoteliers had ways of getting round this. They hoped there were no hidden charges but even if they had only to pay five shillings, the equivalent of two nights' bed and breakfast, it would make a big hole in the money they had to last them for the remainder of the holiday. Anyway they had to eat and looking at the menu given to them by a waiter they chose the roast beef to be followed by apple turnover. The bill including a pot of tea came to ten shillings and sixpence, which they paid and left. They were pleased to have eaten so well but knew that they could not afford to find themselves in such a position again or their money would soon run out; a similar meal in a café at that time would have cost them less than one shilling each.

They struggled on, often having to walk almost a mile before being able to ride and they were too tired after so much walking to make the very short detour of a few miles to say they had been as far as Cornwall. Eventually they came off the moor and taking the main road cycled on until they arrived at the small town of Torrington. Since it was now getting dark they realised they would have to stay in that town for the night. They soon found a very good B&B with friendly owners who entertained them royally. The following morning early, after an excellent breakfast, they set off for the coast, passing through Bideford and Barnstaple and heading across country towards Lynton and Lynmouth, the two beautiful small coastal towns close to Exmoor. The two lads spent some time looking around and then headed east up Countisbury Hill, another very long but beautiful walk pushing the bicycles and resting from time to time to take in the views that opened before them. There was virtually no traffic on the road and when they reached the summit and were able to ride, everything seemed so wonderful and it was hard to imagine there was a war on and that the end of the phoney war, as in later years this first period of the war was called, was almost upon them.

Down Porlock Hill, which was notoriously steep, was where they had to decide whether to take the toll road down, as people in Lynmouth had recommended, or to take the ride down the main road at what undoubtedly would be a breakneck speed to the bottom. Both of them liked the idea of going down hill at high speed but the Lynmouth people had said the ride down on the toll road was very worthwhile, so they opted for the latter and were very pleased they did. The toll road had undoubtedly been built to make it easier for horse-drawn vehicles to climb to the summit and of course provided an income for whoever owned the land on which it had been built. However, it was doubtful if anyone then manned the tollgates and the two boys sailed down and round to the bottom not seeing a soul all the way. The next stop was Minehead where they stayed the night in a B&B and went roller-skating in a covered rink in the town for much of the evening.

The following morning it was off across Exmoor and on to Cheddar Gorge where Bob fell for a beautiful young girl they met. It transpired that she was the daughter of the owner of Gough's Cave and Bob was so smitten that he threatened to call off the holiday and stay down with her. However, he saw sense later in the day and the ride eastwards continued and by nightfall they had reached Bath and another B&B. The following day they set off down the main road towards London, passing the white horse at Marlborough on the way. That evening, Friday, they stayed in Reading and rode back through London to Enfield the next morning, arriving home just after lunch. Both agreed it had been a truly wonderful holiday, they estimated they had travelled over six hundred miles in a week, little realising at the time that if they had delayed their holiday a few more weeks they would have had to travel without the help of signposts, as after Dunkirk all signs that indicated names of towns or villages were removed together with all road signs and the names of railway stations. Don remembered well the chorus of yells that came from soldiers on transports as they were crossing Salisbury Plain, "they'll get you soon" – and get them in the forces they did. Bob was killed less than two years later whilst manning an aircrew rescue launch machine-gunned by a German plane. But this is jumping too far ahead.

Chapter Fourteen

Bob and Don returned to work on the Monday following the holiday, now nearing the end of April 1940. Smithy, who lived locally to Don's office in Tottenham, was called up soon after and joined the RAF to train as aircrew. A few weeks later and the German army broke westwards with the Lufwaffe bombing the Dutch and Belgian towns ahead of them. Most of the French army was behind the Maginot line leaving the border with Belgium and in particular the Ardennes with few troops. The British army went forward into Belgium but were soon forced themselves to retreat. The German army crossed the wooded area of the Ardennes and completely surprised the Allies and there was a real danger that the British expeditionary force would soon be cut off from the sea. Don was able to read in the newspapers and listen to the wireless what a desperate plight the Allies were in. The Germans were moving north to the coast and south towards Paris, and Don had a bet with others in the office that if Paris fell the French would give in. One or two told him he didn't know what he was talking about but within a day or two he was proved right as the French did surrender. The British army with some French had moved to a position on the coast around Dunkirk and, with a rearguard holding back the advancing Germans, awaited evacuation. Over 300,000 men were scattered amongst the dunes on the beaches by Dunkirk and were gradually being rescued by the Royal Navy and hundreds of small boats, which had been called into service to try to bring the soldiers to safety in England. For several terrible days and nights the men were bombed and strafed as they tried to take shelter on the beaches. Eventually it was over and the final tally of soldiers who were safely brought back to England was between three and four hundred thousand. The army of course had suffered a defeat but the evacuation was indeed a victory for the navy and the hundreds of volunteers, seamen and private individuals who had taken part in the rescue.

However, in the face of this disaster it was strange that no one Don knew ever contemplated that Britain would lose the war; yes it was a setback, but Britain and the Empire would of course win in the end, was the general feeling.

It had happened all so quickly and soon the talk was about a possible invasion of the British Isles. The Prime Minister, Neville Chamberlain, resigned and Winston Churchill was appointed in his place. He at once started a series of very uplifting broadcasts on the wireless and he and the government formed what was at first called the Local Defence Volunteers (LDVs), the precursor of the Home Guard. Units were formed in towns and villages all over the country but at that time there were no weapons or uniforms for them and it was common place to see old and young men drilling in civilian clothes armed with any sort of weapon that could be found. Most of the volunteers were men who had fought in the First World War and Don's dad soon volunteered and since he had been commissioned near the end of that war was given the job of officer in charge of the LDV unit that was formed of railway workers based at his depot.

The Royal Air Force (RAF) fighter squadrons, based behind the lines in France, were returned to England as soon as it was evident the Germans would overrun that country and were almost immediately in action over the English Channel, escorting bombers pounding the Germans in France as well as chasing off enemy fighters who themselves were escorting Luftwaffe planes bombing convoys in the Channel.

The Germans had built invasion barges and these were brought to positions along the English Channel coast in France ready for the invasion of England and reports on the wireless regularly told of invasion barges being bombed by the RAF. It was in the bombing of convoys of ships in the English Channel by the Lufwaffe that Don first learnt of the German dive-bomber called the Stuka. The BBC sent a reporter to the south coast to report on one of these battles as seen from the cliffs. His report was broadcast on the wireless and being recorded was sold on a twelve inch 78 in Woolworths. Don bought one for sixpence, which he was able to play on the record player he had bought in his first year at work.

Very soon the Lufwaffe started attacking airfields in England but the RAF fighters, sent up to intercept, soon began taking a heavy toll of both bombers and fighters. For days the blue sky, mainly to the east of London, was covered in vapour trails left by the planes as dogfights were taking place. The sky through most of that summer was beautifully clear and it was easy to see the battles in the air. Both RAF and enemy planes were a common sight flying low over the buildings in north London where Don lived and worked. The air raid shelter behind the small office in Tottenham was visited once or twice by staff but he couldn't remember ever going inside as mostly they all stood outside looking up at the sky and cheering as a Spitfire or Hurricane flashed overhead doing a victory roll.

In the evenings the reports on the wireless always gave the number of enemy and RAF planes shot down, and it became obvious that the RAF were a match for the Luftwaffe. However, at that time the general public were unaware of how serious was the loss of young fighter pilots. Planes were coming off the production lines at a great speed but, although many hundreds of pilots were being trained, the losses of men were putting a severe strain on the service and by September the position was getting serious. It was in this month that the RAF had its greatest success and in one day claimed to have shot down 185 enemy aircraft. After the war the number was shown to have been exaggerated somewhat, but nevertheless the number shot down that day and the few days following was sufficient for the Lufwaffe to decide to change tactics and build up on night bombing.

On a Saturday towards the end of August Don and a few friends decided to take a trolleybus up to London's West End to see a film. They had heard that the film showing at the Paramount, Tottenham Court Road, was worth seeing and although cinemas in town were very much more expensive than the local ones, this one was cheaper than those in Leicester Square, and it would be several weeks before the film would be shown locally. The film was *The Grapes of Wrath* with Henry Fonda. It was as they came out of the cinema that they heard the first bombs on London fall, exactly where they had fallen the boys at that time did not know but Don told his parents they sounded quite close, he remembered it as being 24th August.[*] These were of course the first of many to fall and the heavy bombing of London would shortly go on regularly every night right through the winter until May 10th of the following year, a period known as the Blitz.

The daylight raids began to peter out and it was evident that the daylight battle in the air had been won. This later became known as The Battle of Britain and the RAF had indeed saved the country from invasion, as without control of the air an invasion would have hardly been likely to succeed. The main target for the German bombers at night after August 24th was first to be the London docks, in those days the largest in the World, as indeed was London the largest city in the World with a population of some nine million. Then the raids spread to most areas on the eastern side of the capital both north and south of the river, such as the Lea Valley, where there were scores of factories including the old established armament factory at Enfield Lock famous for the Lee Enfield rifle, then

---

[*] Looking, in the year 2008, at a hand-drawn map of a district of Tottenham, which Don copied from an office map early in 1940 for use in his work, there has been added, obviously at a later date, a note in green ink showing the place where the first bomb landed on Tottenham and the date shown as 24th Aug 1940. So perhaps Tottenham was where the first bomb on London fell?

south of the river to Royal Arsenal at Woolwich, and of course all residential areas within a few miles of these areas. To the west of London the bombing was less severe but no part escaped entirely. The City (the square mile of the old city, the mainly financial centre) later became a particular target where bombs and fire destroyed much.

The Civil Defence forces had the previous year appointed air raid wardens, and fire watch patrols were now formed all over the country. Don joined the one in his street but soon after was transferred to fire watching at his office in Tottenham, such taking precedence over watching at home. The office had lost two of the small staff to the services and to replace them the MWB (his employers) had taken on local retired men, in fact four men were eventually taken on to replace the two young ones.

Chapter Fifteen

Just before the night bombing started, Don Varnier, one of the senior men in the office, approached Don to see if he would help him out with some evening work. This man ran a band that played at small dance halls in north London and as they were beginning to lose men who were being called to the colours, they needed help. The band man, the man in question, knew that Don was someone no one would mess with and he wanted him to look after the door at these dances. His duties would include taking the money for entrance to the dance, making sure everybody paid and, if there were trouble, getting the troublemakers out, in other words he would be a doorkeeper bouncer. He would be paid a share of the takings. Don said he was pleased to do it but he had fire watching at the office. Varnier said he would take care of that with a quiet word to those regularly on duty and get them to allow him, on those nights when on the door of a dance, to arrive late. In fact the firewatchers, all older men, readily agreed to co-operate, especially as they knew Don would be going in the forces eventually and were only too pleased to help.

One of the four older men employed to replace staff lost to the forces whose name was Hardy was immediately nicknamed 'The Judge' after the then famous Hardy films with Mickey Rooney as the star. The 'Judge' was well educated and had run his own business, earning, as he claimed, over a thousand a year, although this was not believed by some in the office as such a sum was almost unheard of in the Water Board at the time. However, the 'Judge' was a good friend to Don, taught him the Morse code and gave him a Morse key and showed him how to use it. The 'Judge' said he had been born on Valentia island off the west coast of Ireland where the first

Morse code messages had been sent across to the USA. The 'Judge' could send and read at some fantastic speed.

The band held regular weekly dances at The Red Lion in Barnet, initially two nights a week, and also at The Robin Hood in Potters Bar for one night, a Friday. Don was at first asked to do one night at Barnet and one at Potters Bar; the Saturday night in Barnet was already policed by two men on the door, so the night Don was to operate he would be on his own.

Barnet, about seven miles from his home, meant he would have to catch a bus for the journey, taking almost half an hour. On his first night he was introduced to the members of the band and shown where he would stand and collect the entrance money. The people in the band were very friendly and he learnt that his work colleague, Varnier, would in fact shortly be the leader of the band as the present leader, who happened to be captain of the St Albans football team, was about to be called into the Services. Varnier played drums and did most of the singing. The charge for the dance was 2/6d (two shillings and six pence or twelve and a half pence in today's money!); in those days a lot of money for a hop, especially as it was possible to get in much bigger halls with well-known bands for less than half that amount. Nevertheless, people rolled up every night and the takings were good. Generally there was no trouble until the bar closed and then there was a rush for the dance hall at the rear, it was at this time that Don had to earn his living and make sure people did not get in without paying – many tried but he reckoned he got them all, either by stopping them at the door or going into the hall and dragging them off the floor. Varnier was well pleased with his new doorkeeper and they soon started a third night at the Barnet venue with Don on the door.

In the early days as doorkeeper/bouncer the Blitz on London was at its height and from the Red Lion, up a small hill in Barnet, one could see the fires and explosions to the south. Of course there were also occasional bombs dropped nearby and on the road back to Enfield, but, as all over the London area, falling shrapnel from the anti-aircraft barrage was one of the most dangerous hazards, it was particularly the case when cycling to and from his other dance venue, The Robin Hood in Potters Bar, so he always carried his tin hat. He particularly liked the latter venue as the publican always royally entertained them after the dance, giving them beer and fresh sandwiches. He always remembered the beer, as although he had only previously tasted beer because all his friends drank it, and then it was either mild and bitter or just bitter, the beer served up by the publican was Taylor Walkers Main Line and after a gruelling night on the door Don always looked forward to his pint and the ham sandwich before he rode the seven miles home on his bicycle, sometimes with his helmet on and other times, if it was reasonably quiet, without.

Varnier, the bandleader, lived in Muswell Hill, which for those unfamiliar with north London is a few miles south of Barnet towards the centre of London, and when the bombing was expected to be heavy Don told his parents he would be staying with his colleague for the night, going straight over to Muswell Hill with Varnier from work.

Varnier drove a motorbike and sidecar and they had to go to his home to pick up the drum kit and then drive to the dancehall. Don was seated in the sidecar and on his lap he had the big base drum and various other bits round his feet, all most uncomfortable. The noise of the bike was deafening, most nights going to the dancehall was generally before the heavy raids started but when returning, often with the bombing at its height, one could see the searchlights, the tracer bullets, bomb bursts and fires but could hardly hear anything above the noise of the bike engine. Varnier drove the bike along at breakneck speed, tearing round corners with Don hanging on to the drum for dear life. Varnier drove as if he were in the Isle of Man TT races, just like Stanley Woods.

Don, on his free nights at this time, particularly on Saturdays, would go along to the library on Enfield Highway and meet his friend Del when he finished work there, the library closing at eight in the evening. From there they would go to a dance and generally find two girls to take home. One week it would be Don's choice and the next Del, the other party having to take the second girl who was not always someone they would normally choose. Often it was a case of having a laugh and, "I don't like yours." Del and Don became very good friends with Del sometimes coming over to Barnet to Don's dancehall.

Chapter Sixteen

One day at the end of Autumn when riding home from work on his bicycle, Don had very bad stomach pains and was pleased to get home. He told his parents that he did not feel very well and before going to bed went to the toilet but once inside collapsed. Fortunately his doctor lived opposite and Don's father rushed over and got him. The doctor immediately went back to his house and telephoned for an ambulance. Eventually the ambulance came and took Don to the North Middlesex Hospital in Edmonton where he was operated on straightaway for an acute appendicitis, it was about midnight.

Operations in those days meant you were kept in bed and so Don was in hospital for nearly two weeks without getting out of bed. The Blitz was at its height and whilst in there the hospital was bombed and, nearby, a number of landmines were dropped on a packed residential area, flattening hundreds of Victorian terraced houses and killing and wounding many inhabitants. The hospital, no more than a half a mile from the nearest landmine, got off lightly that time, being hit only with scores of incendiary bombs, which were put out by staff armed with buckets and stirrup pumps thus saving patients and wards, but no one was able to save the hospital chapel which was badly burned. Each night the staff moved the beds into the centre of the wards to keep patients away from the glass windows and when incendiaries landed staff could be seen running backwards and forwards carrying buckets of water and wielding stirrup pumps. Don and others in the ward hardly had any sleep but lots of laughs.

It was whilst Don was off from work with his appendicitis that four of his friends, Bob, Del, Eric, and Bill, went together and volunteered for RAF aircrew.

The weeks went by and Don carried on with his job in Tottenham whilst for three evenings, later four, a week acted as doorkeeper/bouncer at the dances. On his free evenings he often met up with the gang, going with them to local dances or cinemas and occasionally entertaining them in his home when the whole group would play cards with his dad or, as his parents had recently bought the new game Monopoly – costing ten shillings (a day's wages for the average manual worker) – this too proved very popular with all. The big night of the week of course was Saturday and since his friend Del mostly worked late in the library on this night, Don continued to meet him outside his branch in Enfield Wash, before going out for the evening. Mostly they went ballroom dancing, the main pursuit of the young at this time, and there were always plenty of dance halls from which to choose. Don and his friends mostly frequented local halls but occasionally went further afield. Thus one Saturday the venue chosen was a hall in Palmers Green, a trolleybus ride away, and it was here that Don met a young girl and seeing her home that night arranged to meet her again on one of his free nights in the following week. So far it seemed none of the gang had regular girlfriends and they pulled Don's leg when he told them he was seeing the girl again. However, meeting with the girl did not last long, as Don learnt that not only was she already engaged to a soldier overseas but hinted to him she would break this off if Don were serious over her. He certainly did not want to get tied down and gently broke it off with the girl.

Whilst at the dance hall in Palmers Green they learnt that one could go dancing there on Sundays providing one joined the club. In 1940 activities on Sundays were few and far between, all shops were closed and the only places of entertainment were some cinemas that generally showed 'old' films on the few hours they were open. Thus discovering the Sunday dance was of interest to Don and certain of his friends. Having a club was of course simply a way of getting round the law, which did not permit you to pay for this entertainment on a Sunday in the normal way. So Don and the gang joined, paying the fee and adding this hall as a meeting place over the next few Sunday afternoons. Bombs were falling on London every night and, although this did not stop the boys going out in the evenings, to find a place of entertainment on a Sunday was a bonus.

He still cycled to work whenever he could, but occasionally the weather was too bad and he was forced to go by train. It was nearing Christmas 1940 when on one such journey by train he met an old school friend who told him there was to be an all night party at a house in Edmonton and the girls there were looking for a few fellows to go along. Don said he would like to go and would try and bring one or two others with him. He managed to persuade some friends and they agreed to meet up at the Cross Keys public house on Edmonton Green to have a couple of drinks before turning up at the party to be held close by.

Early on the evening for the party, Don and friends duly met at the Cross Keys. The atmosphere in the pub was quite lively and even the air raid siren sounding and the sound of guns firing made no difference. People had got used to the nightly bombing although some, particularly those living closer to the centre of London, went to shelters, most took their chance and tried to carry on life as if there were no bombing. Don and his friends were so enjoying themselves they almost forgot their reason for coming until one of their number said, "I think we have had enough, if we are going to the party we better leave soon."

The others nodded agreement and after one final drink they left.

The house, one of many late Victorian-terraced houses that filled the roads near to the pub, was soon found and Don and his friends, really in no fit state to arrive at a party, opened the small iron gate and walked the two steps to the front door and knocked. A young lady answered the door and immediately asked them to come in. They followed her into the front room of the small house, known usually as the parlour, and found within four other girls, an older lady and gentleman, which they assumed to be the parents, and a young lad of perhaps fourteen. The young lady who had answered the door, Sylvia, was the host, the eldest child of the two parents in the room; the young lad was her brother. The boys were introduced to all present and the party got under way. A radiogram in the corner of the room was playing well-known music with records being changed automatically under the watchful eye of the young lad. The noise in the room gradually increased as girls and boys mixing well got to know each other.

Don liked the look of one girl he had spotted but before he had a chance of engaging her in conversation one of the other lads seemed to have laid claim. Don satisfied himself with talking to the hostess and her parents, both of whom joined in the game of charades that was introduced when more drink and food had been consumed. The game carried on for a long time. Later card games developed and still Don had his eye on the girl he had first wanted to talk to, but all he was able to get was her name and that she went dancing at weekends at St Stephen's hall in Bush Hill Park. The drinking and games continued for several hours until some gave up and lying down on the floor fell asleep. Just before dawn broke the familiar 'All Clear' siren sounded and people decided it was time to go home. Some of the fellows walked to the station to catch a train back to Enfield while Don, who lived just over a mile away, walked home. The young ladies who lived nearby the party house stayed on for breakfast.

Chapter Seventeen

Don meets Betty

The following Saturday Don as usual met his friends over
Burtons at the Spot Club and eventually persuaded them to go
along to the dance at St Stephens where he hoped he would see
the girl he had seen at the party. They had not been there long
when he spotted her talking to two other girls and as soon as
the bandleader announced the next dance he walked swiftly
over and asked her for a dance. He found they talked easily to
each other and from then on he managed to have most of the
remaining dances with her and especially the last waltz where
it was the usual or opportune time for the man to ask to see the
young lady to her home. Her name was Betty and sure enough
she agreed, warning that it was a good walk and that her friend
Sylvia would walk along with them. Don said he didn't mind,
as he just wanted to get to know her more.

He walked along between the two young ladies and during
the walk of about a mile and half a number of planes passed
overhead and anti-aircraft guns nearby opened up.

"I shan't be sorry to go back tomorrow," Betty said.

"Go back where?" Don asked.

"Oh, I was thinking you were told at the party. I go back to
the country – I work for a company who have been evacuated
from the City. We work in a big country mansion in
Bedfordshire and live in huts in the ground. I only come home
now and again to see the family."

She went on to tell him she was a telephonist for an
insurance company previously in Threadneedle Street but now
in a little village called Silsoe.

"I still work up in town," her friend said, "I wish we had been evacuated."

They carried on walking and talking and just after Betty said she lived in the house just in front of them Sylvia said she would say goodnight as she lived just a little further along. Don offered to see her to her home but she said it was no distance and that she would be home in a couple of minutes. They both said goodnight to the friend and carried on talking outside the typical Victorian end of a terrace house of three floors.

They must have talked for half an hour, she telling him about life in the country and he giving her a few facts about where he worked and had gone to school. It was near midnight when he left, suggesting they should meet again sometime but no date was fixed. They shook hands and Betty let herself in to the house and Don began his long walk home.

On the way home there were a few more planes overhead with the usual anti-aircraft gunfire and one or two bombs dropped a mile or so away. Little did Don know then that the dance hall he had recently been frequenting in Palmers Green had been bombed that night. He learnt of this the following morning when his friend Ron came round to see if he was alright; Ron knew Don had been going regularly to that hall and felt sure his friend had been there when the bomb had fallen. It seemed that about thirty people were killed in the hall and on the trolleybus passing at the time.

"I most certainly would have been going there but for wanting to see a girl I met at the party and learning she would be at St Stephen's," he told Ron.

Later that morning he went for a walk with his cousin Harry and after lunch suddenly decided to ride round to Betty's house and see whether she would come out for a ride. He knocked on the front door and a lady, obviously Betty's mother, opened it.

"I was wondering if Betty was home?"

"Yes, she is in the garden cleaning her bicycle. Walk round the side and go into the garden, you'll find her down the bottom."

He thanked the lady and walked round as instructed and down to the end of the garden.

Betty saw him coming and blushed bright red, obviously being worried what he might think, seeing her in old clothes with dirty hands and no make-up. Don realised she was somewhat embarrassed and immediately asked her if she would like to come out for a ride.

"I'll help you finish off cleaning the bike if you'll come."

Betty, having got over the shock of seeing him, said later that she was inwardly pleased as she liked him and had indeed wished he had asked her last evening for a date.

"Yes I would like to come, the bike is finished anyway. Let me go indoors and change my clothes and I will be with you in five minutes. I'll see you outside. Would you wheel my bike round please."

Don wheeled the bike out through the gate and waited. It was not long before Betty appeared and mounting their bikes rode off up Church Street to the Cambridge Road. The Cambridge Road was then a relatively new road with cycle tracks on either side, the only road Don knew that had them, so they rode on these although since there was hardly any traffic on the main road they could easily have ridden along it in complete safety. It was quite a long ride to get out into the country and as it was already quite late in the afternoon they did not attempt to go too far but finding a seat by the roadside sat down and talked. Both found it easy to make conversation and soon agreed they would like to meet again. However, Betty said she had to go back to Silsoe the following morning and would not be able to come home the next weekend, as she would be on duty.

"So I shan't see you for at least two weeks," Don said, "You better give me your address and I'll write you a letter..." he hesitated, "That's if you would like me to?"

"Of course I would. I want your address too."

They rode back to her house and exchanged addresses and then he asked her if she would like to go out that evening to the pictures and she said she would.

Thus began a close relationship with both writing letters to each other in the periods between Betty's visits to her home. One weekend when Betty was on duty it was agreed that Don go up on the Sunday to see her. He was given detailed instructions on how to get there, Betty saying she would meet him at the bus station in Luton, and so after looking up the time of the trains and buses they arranged to meet at 10.30. He had to take a train from his home station, Bush Hill Park, up to Liverpool Street, which reminded him of his daily journeys to school about four years earlier. He found the journey had not changed, St Paul's cathedral still managed to change from one side of the carriage to the other and the train stopped at every station. Then it was on the underground to St Pancras where he was to catch a train to Luton. He had never been on St Pancras station before although it was quite close to where he had worked at the head office of the Water Board the previous year. On entering the station he immediately noticed the road running along by one of the platforms and he was reminded of his dad telling him of the time he was fireman on the Royal Train, which left that station to take the royal party to Sandringham. Sandringham Station was in fact on the London and North Eastern Railway with the London terminus being Liverpool Street, but since the latter station had no road close to a platform so that the royal family's carriage and horses could drive up close to the train, St Pancras had to be used, even though trains from that station did not go to Sandringham, it belonging to a rival company, the London Midland and Scottish railway, or LMS as it was known. Of course his dad's engine and train were LNER rolling stock, the train crossing over to the LNER main line shortly after leaving St Pancras.

Don crossed the road and made his way to the platform for Luton.

He had never been on an LMS train and of course the line to Luton was all new to him and he eagerly tried to read the names of the stations as the train sped through, he remembered a place called Radlett but most of the other station names were quite new to him and it was not long before they were rolling in to Luton station.

It was a bright sunny day, although still only February, and leaving the station soon found his way to the bus station where he spotted Betty waiting.

This was the first time he had ever travelled to see a girl and not being in the familiar surroundings of where he lived he was strangely apprehensive.

"Have you been here long?" he ventured.

"No, I have only just arrived. That's our bus over there, the one I came on, we've got about ten minutes before it is due to return to Bedford."

The village to where Betty's company had been evacuated was about ten miles north of Luton, a village called Silsoe, about halfway on the road to Bedford. The two young people went upstairs on the bus and sat in the front seat so that, Betty said, he could see the countryside which had become so familiar to this young lady. However, having got over the slight embarrassment at the first meeting on unfamiliar territory they had so much to say to each other that Don did not take as much notice of the countryside as he should, although he said afterwards he did remember seeing some pretty country near a village called Barton, about half way along the road.

"Oh yes that's right, it is nice there, its full name is Barton in the Clay."

The bus stop in Silsoe was quite close to the impressive gates of the mansion where Betty worked and which had been her home since she joined the company soon after war had been declared. They walked through the gate and up the very long drive to the house, Betty pointing out on the far side of the house the many huts where most of the staff lived. The house itself was mainly used as offices and she took Don in and showed him the telephone room where she worked as a telephonist, one of two girls who operated an eyeball switchboard. She then showed him her private little section in one of the huts, known by staff as a cubicle, and then took him for lunch to a small cottage in the village. After lunch she gave him a guided tour of the lovely grounds of the house, known as Wrest Park. He later read in a book that the house had been famous for the glamorous parties held just before and after 1900, a house mentioned by Winston Churchill in one of his books as a place he often visited when young. It was the first time Don had ever been into the grounds of a big country mansion and was most impressed by what he saw, although he learnt later that the lake, the orangery, the fountains and of course the pretty bridge over a stream, were generally common with many grand houses and probably copied or designed by Capability Brown.

The day went all too quickly and after kissing Betty goodbye he caught the bus back to Luton and on to home and so to work on Monday.

The date for call-up registration for the services had come round a month or so after Don had returned to work following his time in hospital, in fact just before he met Betty, and as his friends had done, when he was in hospital, he too had volunteered for aircrew. Later that year his friends, Bob, Del, Eric and Bill were called for their two medicals early in 1941 and were all to find themselves in the RAF before the year ended. Don was called for his first medical in the spring but, having ticked Rheumatic Fever on the medical form handed to him, was told he would have to see a heart specialist before he could be accepted

The Blitz on London had continued night after night, but none of the family used the shelter he and his dad had built in the garden at the time of the Munich Crisis, instead they took their chance in the house. They were extremely lucky as every night the bombers came and many bombs fell in the area; in fact one evening when he was at home there was a knock on the door which, after making sure the lights would not shine outside, he opened, to be faced by a man in great distress. Don did not recognise the man who at once announced who he was.

"I'm your dad's fireman; I have just been bombed out." The man was crying and Don asked him to come in and closed the door. He took the man into the room where his parents were listening to the wireless. His dad spoke, "What's up, Fred?"

"We've just been bombed out, the house is flattened, luckily me and the wife were in the shelter, she's alright and staying with a neighbour. I thought I ought to tell you as I don't think I can come to work tonight, could you get someone to take my place?"

"Oh I am so sorry, Fred, that's dreadful, come and sit down a bit, I'll go over to the station later and get them to ring through to Enfield and tell them what's happened. We thought we heard a big one close by, I guess that must have been the one that hit your house. Bloody Germans, I hope our boys give them hell."

Don's dad's fireman, or mate, as they were generally known, stayed for a while, had a cup of tea and then said he would be going back.

"You can stay here if you like, Fred."

"No thanks, Bert, I'll go back and see the missus – the neighbour up the road said we can stay there until we get settled somewhere. I'll probably see you tomorrow night."

Of course this sort of thing was happening all around this part of north London, however, it was the City (i.e. the old square mile covering the financial district), the East End and docks that bore the brunt of the attacks. Although no one knew at the time, the Blitz on London was to continue until one final heavy raid on May 10th 1941 when suddenly the continual nightly raids stopped. This was the time the Germans invaded Russia and obviously Hitler needed much of the Lufwaffe to support the millions of men he threw into that campaign. Of course the Lufwaffe continued to bomb London but less frequently and none of these subsequent raids were to match the nine months of the Blitz.

Chapter Eighteen

It was several weeks after his first medical that Don was called to see a Harley Street specialist, and travelling by bus and underground soon found the appropriate house in the well-known street. A lady opened the door and took him straight in to see the specialist, a middle-aged gentleman who asked him a few questions and then proceeded to put him through a series of tests, including immersing his feet in water, linked, Don believed, to an electric current. Some time later the man asked him if he really wanted to go into the forces, hinting he had reasons to fail him. Don quickly dispelled these thoughts from the man's mind telling him all his friends had gone into aircrew and he wanted to follow them.

"Very well, young man, I will pass you."

Don went home and awaited being called for the second medical, known as the aircrew medical.

In the meantime he continued his doorkeeping job and during the week meeting up with friends not yet called to the colours, whilst reserving his weekends for Betty when she was home. On Saturdays he had managed to play a few games of football for his Old Boys who had arranged a few fixtures. The Water Board teams (Aquarius) he had played so well for before war was declared, drew players from all different parts of London, and had found it difficult to get fixtures or people to play, and of course it would have been foolish for Don to think of travelling across London to the home ground south of the river whilst the bombing of London was so heavy.

At work Smithy had left to join the RAF and, not long after, the Navy had called George. The boss told Don he would have to take over the work George had left since the four retired gentlemen, employed to fill the gap, could not be expected to do the walking the outside work required. Thus Don had been doing a senior's job, but of course without it being reflected in his pay. George had looked after a large section of the borough of Tottenham and Don had to become familiar with this. He was responsible for seeing rates were collected from bad payers and to check the district for houses empty or bombed so that it was known from whom rates were expected. It might seem strange to some reading this book to worry about collecting water rates and virtually carry on as before the war even though factories, shops and houses were continually under attack. But of course water was most important and the men who worked in the pumping stations, or repaired damaged water pipes, or examined water quality, or indeed worked in the offices to collect rates, had all to be paid wages and without rates being paid there would be none.

He soon became familiar with his allotted district after he drew himself a map, by copying from a big one of Tottenham they had on the wall in the office, drawing it freehand, as in those days there were no copying machines.

In May 1940 Don had been appointed to the permanent staff of the Water Board after a year and a half as a temporary, his salary increasing from 27/6d a week to £90 per annum. Now a year later it went up to £110 per annum, almost two pounds a week! Actually he was earning more each week in his doorkeeper job than he earned by working for the Water Board five and half days a week; he was indeed a rich young man often taking over five pounds a week, nearly twice that earned by many men in full-time employment.

It was about this time that he developed a raging toothache and his under boss suggested that he should have his teeth checked by his son who was training to be a dentist at the National Dental Hospital in London. It has to be remembered that dental care was not at that time taken so seriously as it was to be in later years. If you had toothache you went to the dentist and he pulled out the offending tooth; filling was rare and of course was without anaesthetic. Don had one or two other decayed teeth so when he was told he could go in work time to this London hospital, plus that the cost would be negligible, it was arranged he would go.

He travelled to the hospital in Great Portland Street by trolleybus and underground in mid-1941 and after paying sixpence was shown into a large room with many dentists' chairs in rows, some occupied and some empty. He was introduced to his under boss's son, Gordon, who now would have a new patient on whom to practise what he had learnt. A qualified dentist gave him a cursory examination and passed him over to Gordon who he had met once before at the party arranged by the lady who worked in Don's office.

It was a painfully slow process getting Don's teeth fixed and he began visiting the hospital once or twice a week. It usually took two or three visits to drill and fill a tooth, Gordon doing his best to avoid paining Don too much, there were of course no injections for filling teeth in those days. However, it was soon discovered that the tooth causing him pain from time to time had an abscess growing on the root and it was decided by the resident dental surgeon that he would perform an operation in front of the other students, which Don heard was called an apus sectomy. This time he was given a local anaesthetic and the root of the tooth cut in order to drain the abscess, all the time the surgeon was explaining to the students what he was doing. Don was told he would have to come back to allow the abscess to drain when the surgeon would crown the tooth, something that Don had never heard of before. Each visit was charged at sixpence but when Don returned for the crowning, a week or so later, he had to pay an extra 2/6d for the amalgam post the surgeon would use to fix the crown; there was no National Health at the time. He continued going to the hospital over the next few months and became known to most of the students, both male and female; Gordon said they knew him as the star crown patient. He became such a frequent visitor that he had told his parents they treated him like a member of staff and thus it came as no surprise when Charing

Cross Hospital, with which they were associated, could not field a full football team, he was asked if he would play; Gordon's father had obviously told his son of Don's exploits when playing for Aquarius. He of course agreed and having previously played against one of the other students, Peter, whilst they were at school, he, Gordon and Don went off to play for the Hospital. It was not long after playing there that Don was offered the opportunity of playing for Barnet FC; again Don's under boss had been the catalyst and must have told Lester Finch, the England amateur international who later played for Wolves, of his 1939 rapid progress to the first team of Aquarius playing in the well-respected Southern Amateur and Nemean Leagues. Don had only a few games with Barnet but the pull of seeing Betty for as long as possible on the weekends she was home was too great and he gave up playing, particularly as sometimes when the fixture was away from home he would get back so late that half the evening was gone. He was always conscious that he might not be around much longer.

It was about this time that he was able to introduce Betty to his parents when he arranged to meet them in a public house near to his home. The meeting was successful and his parents seemed to approve.

Then his friend Ron asked him if he would be best man at his wedding. Don did not know anything about being a best man but was assured he had nothing to do and thus took on the job and took Betty with him to the church in Enfield Town and later to Glad, Ron's wife's, home.

He no doubt did his job but not quite the way he later learned was expected of a best man, he was only just eighteen.

Early in December 1941 the Americans were forced to enter the war when the Japanese raided Pearl Harbour. Of course it was good to have the Americans on our side but neither Betty nor Don mentioned it in their letters and this seemed to reinforce the notion that the British people did not think the

Americans would make that much difference as they were going to win anyway.

Later that month he received the date for his appointment for the second RAF aircrew selection medical, it was to be early in January.

Christmas 1941 came and Don spent Christmas Day at home but on Boxing Day he was invited to the family party held at Betty's house. He had never before been to such a party and he undoubtedly envied her for the big friendly family she had, nearly all the aunts and uncles and their many children living within a mile of her mother's house. Don was the only young man there, the uncles being of First World War vintage, and he felt how lucky he was to still be around. It was at this party that he first realised how Churchill's speeches on the wireless were generally raising morale as people at the party made several references to them. In particular he remembered a lot of laughter when one of the uncles impersonating said "...Some chicken. Some neck."

Bob, Del, Eric and Bill had now all gone into the RAF and here was Don still a civilian, although not for long he thought. But how wrong can you be!

In January he attended the RAF selection board in Euston and passed the written tests which included maths, general knowledge etc., and told he would be accepted for training as a pilot, but then came the medical which he was sure he would pass and indeed was doing well in this until he came to the eyes, ears and nose specialist. This man, after asking him unsuccessfully to breathe through one nostril, examined the nose further and said it was completely blocked on one side and that he would have to have an operation to clear it before he could accept him for aircrew.

"You must have had a heavy blow on your nose to cause such a blockage. How did this happen?"

"It must have been a fight I had in a fairground before the war," Don replied.

"Well the only way you will get into aircrew is to have an operation on your nose. Go away and when you have had it, report back."

His mother thought he was mad to try and get the operation, as she obviously did not want him to go into aircrew. He wrote to tell Betty what had happened and she was pleased that at least he would be around for a while longer. He went to his doctor to tell him what was to happen and he said he would help him find a hospital but told him it would not be easy as most were heavily involved in war casualties. Don was first sent to The Prince of Wales Hospital in Tottenham but they did not have any spare beds, however, the specialist did say, as the RAF wanted him to have the operation, that he would do his best to find a hospital.

It was a couple months later that he was sent to a hospital in Wanstead and the operation was carried out under a local anaesthetic, the surgeon hammering away at the offending bone. Don did feel some pain and the ward sister who attended the operation spoke to him when he was back in the ward.

"Did that hurt you, Ginger?"

He said he did feel some pain.

"I thought you did as I could see your feet moving, I told the surgeon but he took no notice."

Don was in hospital a week and Betty came to see him there when she was home at the weekend.

Out of hospital he reported back to Air Ministry that he had had the operation. Once again he was called to Euston and had another medical examination and passed. He was formally accepted into the RAF, given a number and an RAFVR (RAF Volunteer Reserve) badge, but told that as there were so many waiting to be trained as pilots he would be put on deferred leave, which would be about five months.

Chapter Nineteen

He wore the tiny badge in his lapel but of course hardly anyone knew what it was. As mentioned before, his job entailed going out of the office and either checking for empty houses or trying to collect rates from bad payers. Amongst the worse payers were small shops who ignored the notices and letters sent to them, some deliberately waiting for someone to come round and collect, others even then making excuses or saying they had already paid. Many of the shopkeepers in Tottenham were Jewish and although most were very friendly greeting you as a long lost friend, "How are you, nice to see you, we wondered when you would be coming around," there were those who were downright awkward and it was as much as Don could do to hold his temper. As an example of this and how useless the badge was, came about when he called on a Jewish barber in West Green Road; Don quietly asked the man for his rates – he had already sent him three notices as was the practice before calling – but the man obviously did not want to pay. Don found it was quite common for people to say, "Water comes from the skies, why should we pay water rates?" ... how they thought it was purified and got into their taps he never knew. This particular individual was a very nasty type but Don held his temper until the man said in front of two or three customers in a loud voice, "You ought to be in the forces." That did it. Don had to restrain himself from knocking the man over but instead pointed to his badge and said, "I am already in the RAF, this badge is an RAF Volunteer Reserve badge and if you don't take back what you said, I'll come round here after work and see you." Don was very angry and with red hair was quite capable of acting when aroused. Fortunately the man realised he had gone too far and sheepishly said he was sorry, went to his cash till and took out the money for the rates. What the other men in the barber's shop thought Don could only guess. He left the shop still shaking with anger and walking on to his next call thought how different were people. There were those who happily often queued to pay their rates on the first notice sent to them, others who waited until the red notice was received before paying, whilst there were those who waited for the notice threatening to cut off their water supply or threatening legal action against them before paying, and then finally there were those who ignored all the notices and waited for a call to be made to their abode, most of whom then paid but some who even then tried to hold out, either being taken to court or having their water cut off and incurring extra charges for turning it on again. The extra cost incurred in delayed payments was not insignificant and Don knew that but for this rates could no doubt have been reduced. He concluded therefore that the test of when a citizen paid generally decided who good citizens were and who were not.

Thus work for the Water Board and Don's evening work continued through some months in 1942. His friends who had joined earlier were, with one exception, already well on their way to becoming pilots having nearly completed their training in Canada. The one exception was Bob, the friend he had gone on holiday with during the phoney war. Bob had not made it as a pilot and had gone on Air Sea Rescue and based, Don thought, up in Scotland.

Some weeks passed and then late one evening his friend Ron called at the house with the devastating news that Bob had been killed. He told Don that the airman killed on the Air Sea Rescue launch, as reported on the wireless that evening, had been his friend Bob. Don remembered the report on the wireless had stated that an RAF fighter ace, Paddy Finucane, had been reported missing over the sea, and that an Air Sea Rescue launch searching for him had been attacked by a Messerschmitt and one of the crew of the launch had been killed. They carried on to say that RAF launches rescued both

German and RAF crews who had been forced to ditch in the sea and it was intimated that attacking such a vessel was no different from attacking a Red Cross ambulance.

Bob was brought home to Enfield and buried there with full military honours, among the pall bearers were Bob's and Don's Enfield friends in the RAF – Don wanted to be among them but Bob's father only wanted men in uniform. Don was inwardly upset as he had done his best to join the RAF and it was not his fault that he had not yet been called.

It was not long after that he learnt that his old friend Del had been injured whilst training in the RAF and was in hospital in Ely. Don decided to pay him a visit one Sunday and when he told Ron, who himself was in the RAF but in a quiet number in London, he said he would like to come along as he could get a pass that day. They found they could get a slow train from Enfield Lock station, which was on the main line to Cambridge, and arriving in Ely later that morning they soon found the RAF hospital and Del with his leg in plaster. As it was near lunch time Del suggested they go over to the mess to get something to eat. Don pointed out that he was not in uniform but Del said if anyone asks you say you are from Cardington on a spot of leave. "Anyway no one is going to bother you," he said; of course Don should have known that to say that was an invitation for something to happen, and sure enough it did.

They had not been seated long when an RAF padre came over and sat next to them and soon asked Don where he was from. Don duly said Cardington and the padre said, "Oh I know Cardington well." He then proceeded to ask some very awkward questions which Don managed to counter but for a while it was most embarrassing and he was certainly glad to get out of that airmen's mess.

Chapter Twenty

Engaged and into the RAF

Thus time passed and Don and Betty got engaged, Don buying the ring with Betty in a shop in South Tottenham. But the call-up after the five months did not come and indeed several more weeks passed before it happened. His friends in the RAF were passing out – two as sergeant pilots and one, Del, as a pilot officer. In the meantime Don had joined the ATC (Air Training Corp) with one of his friends also waiting for his papers but in all they only attended the lectures once a week, both lads being too busy to go more, particularly knowing that before very long they would be in the real thing.

When his calling-up papers eventually arrived he had to report to Lords Cricket Ground in London which had become the reception centre for all potential aircrew trainees. He had been to the ground once before when at school to see one day of a test match between England and the West Indies. A small party of boys had gone to the match to watch Kenneth Farnes the England fast bowler who had been at the same school as Don, leaving when Don joined. Of course arriving at Lords now was not quite the same. He with many others were soon issued with uniforms and allocated to one of the various blocks of flats nearby which had been taken over by the RAF. Then came the first square bashing, or rather street bashing, followed by floor scrubbing and seemingly everything to make sure that the new recruits knew how insignificant and unimportant they were. The following day they had to parade early, while it was still dark, and were marched down to a swimming pool at Seymour Hall about a mile or so distance. Here they were introduced to dinghy drill, having to jump off the top board wearing a Mae West life jacket. A number of lads had never been in a pool or in water to swim and it must have been tough for some, one lad taking an awful lot of persuading to climb up and jump. As expected the sergeant showed no mercy for any and seemed to enjoy shouting and hurrying the boys up the steps in their wet life jackets, where on his order one jumped. "Number one, ready, jump; number two, ready, jump," and so on.

The marching round the streets continued day after day and undoubtedly the marching soon improved and even the awkward boys were soon keeping in step and bringing their feet down together with everyone else on the halt. The weeks passed and Christmas came and dinner was taken in the Regents Park zoo nearby, most of the animals of course having been removed to Whipsnade, a zoo that had been opened in the Hertfordshire countryside not long before the war.

Don in January had his birthday and was given guard duty that same day; it was just the way things were. However, a few weeks into the course when many of the young lads were feeling pretty down, something happened that Don was sure helped to cheer them up. Remember he, due to the delay over his medical problems, was three years older than most of the lads and things did not seem to bother him as it did some of the young ones. It was one evening and the chores for the day were over and most of the lads were up in their rooms. Suddenly someone came along the corridor outside shouting, "AC2 Moggs to report to the Commanding Officer." Don went out into the corridor and met the lad shouting his name and asked him what it was all about, but the messenger had no idea. So Don went down the stairs and found the CO's office and knocked on the door and entered. He marched up to the desk, behind which an officer was seated, and saluted. Then out of the corner of his eye he saw another officer sitting in an easy chair and turning he saw it was his old pal Del. Del had come along to take him out on the town. Del wore a raincoat and thus it was not possible to know whether he was a wing commander or merely a pilot officer. Anyway the CO seemed to be treating him as at least an equal and Del had got Don a late pass for that night. However, before leaving to do the town, Don persuaded Del to come up to meet the lads who he said needed cheering up. He knew that Del was quite capable of doing this and agreed. As they entered the room all present jumped up from what they were doing and came to attention, but Del quickly put them at their ease and began to tell them that what they were going through would soon end and that the corporals and sergeants they now seemed to fear were only doing their job and they would find when they were posted they would become quite friendly. He told them one or two stories of what it would be like later on in their training before taking Don out for the night. Don was sure that the next day the flight Del had talked to had more of a 'devil may care attitude' than they had had before meeting his friend.

The evening with Del was a great success and Don would always remember it. They started off the evening by going to the pictures, to see the new big film that had just arrived in the West End, *Casablanca*. It was showing at the Warner Theatre in Leicester Square. It was particularly memorable for many of the audience standing up and singing when Paul Henreid led the singing of the Marsellaise in Humphrey Bogart's café in the film.

They followed the cinema by going to a nightclub. Del told him that the previous night he had flown over the Alps to bomb the port of Genoa – Don thought it all seemed so unreal.

The time came for his flight to be posted, all except one member were told they were going to an ITW (Initial Training Wing) in Babbacombe, Devon, the odd one being one of the lads Del had talked to that night, a lad who, although only eighteen, had made a name for himself playing rugby. His name was Bleddyn Williams and his posting was to an ITW in Cambridge undoubtedly so whilst there he could play rugby for the university. Don never met him again and a year later saw his photograph in the *Tatler*, the writing under the photo said

"Pilot Officer Bleddyn Williams with Air Marshall…" – good in sport certainly let you meet the right people. Bleddyn became Welsh rugby captain after the war.

The journey to ITW was memorable, the train from Paddington arriving at Torquay station on a sunny afternoon with the palm trees near the station making the whole place look like the French Riviera. A sergeant met the train and ordered the new arrivals to form up on the street outside with full packs in preparation for the march to wherever. The flight marched smartly through Torquay and up the rising ground to Babbacombe, quite a tough march with full packs. They were halted outside a private house, opposite a small hotel, which was to be their home for the next several months.

The training was to be quite extensive, plenty of classes and lots of marching and other outside activities. There were several other flights in Babbacombe and great rivalry between them spurred on by the sergeant in charge of Don's flight. All in all every day except Sundays Don and his colleagues were kept busy marching, running and sitting in class; subjects in class included armaments, theory of flight, navigation, Morse code including use of the Aldis lamp, meteorology, aircraft recognition, etc. Outdoors apart from marching and arms drill etc. there were long runs, football on the beach and clay pigeon shooting. Mixed in with all this were periods of guard duty, guarding headquarters, and various places in the town used by the RAF.

Don had one guard duty outside headquarters when the officers were having a party and it was just his luck to be there when they arrived with their wives or girlfriends. One had to salute the officers and their ladies and carrying a rifle this meant looking at their rank as certain senior ranks require different salutes. Don was glad when his two-hour sojourn ended. On another occasion he had to stand guard outside a garage in the middle of the night; and in the middle of a pitch-black night, about two in the morning, Don heard someone approaching. He immediately shouted, "Halt! Who goes there?" and shone his shaded torch towards the footsteps and saw a man who when asked produced his identity card and said he was not sure of his road back into Torquay having just taken a young lady home. Don directed him and returned to his guard duty. Shortly after another person approached and this time it turned out to be a policeman who warned Don to be on the lookout as it was rumoured that a submarine had dropped enemy agents along the coast. Don thought of the man he had so recently directed into Torquay, but he thought better of it and never said anything, but he has often wondered!

Don was down in Babbacombe for about five months and nearing the end of this time the coast from Babbacombe to Paignton suffered an unexpected raid by German FW90s, their latest fighter bombers. It was on a Sunday and Don had joined a party visiting Buckfast Abbey arranged by one of the padres. The party travelled by buses and it was on the return journey whilst changing buses at Newton Abbott they got the news that there had been an air raid in the Torquay area. When they got back to Babbacombe and saw the damage along the cliff tops they realised the raid had been quite severe. Of course there were scores of aircrew out and about on the beaches and cliffs, it being Sunday, when the raid happened and many said they saw the planes coming and at first thought they were RAF Typhoons, which in silhouette were very similar, but they soon realised the error when they flashed overhead firing cannon shells, machine guns and dropping bombs. Most buildings along the cliff tops were badly damaged, including the headquarter building, and a church in St Marychurch had been hit and 28 children and their teacher had been killed; today over a porch into the church there is an inscription stating this fact. It seems the German planes had flown low over the Channel, below the Radar screen, and then proceeded to drop bombs and fire cannon shells all along the sea fronts from Babbacombe, through Torquay to Paignton. A number of airmen and civilians had also been killed.

At a dance in the local town hall in St Marychurch a week later an announcement was made thanking the soldier who had manned the machine gun emplacement over the toilet block on the seafront, and had remained at his post firing at the planes as they swept one after the other along the seafront.

A day or so after this raid Don's sister came down to spend a few days on holiday and hopefully see her brother. He had arranged for her to stay at a house in Babbacombe where the parents of one of the members of his flight lived. Don had written to tell her to report to the headquarters building for directions to the house but of course on arriving she found this was no longer occupied. However, she eventually found where to go and managed to see Don on one or two evenings and on the Saturday went with him to a tea dance in Torquay.

A week or so later the flight left Torquay by train for Derby. Don was the only one to have anyone see them off at the station, in the person of a young lady on holiday from Birmingham, whom he had met at a dance, who came along to wave the boys off. From Derby station they were taken to an airfield outside town at a place called Burnaston.[*]

---

[*] Burnaston is no longer an airfield and now houses a factory making Toyota cars.

Chapter Twenty-One

The course at Burnaston was called a Grading Course where the intention was to begin to see who was suited to be a pilot. Each were given twelve hours' flying instruction and assessed as to suitability or otherwise. Many soloed in that time, although if you did not it did not mean you would not continue on a pilot's course. In fact Don soloed after eleven hours flying. One member of his flight on his solo flight scared everyone by going round thirteen times before he made a very bumpy landing. Long before he had landed all flying was stopped and the fire engine and blood wagon were called out. Don lost touch with this lad but doubted whether he was picked for pilot training.

From Burnaston Don and his friends were posted to Manchester, to await shipment overseas. At first he was put in a flat with three other fellows at the top of a house in Salford. Whilst there during the day they had to take a short ride on a tram to Heaton Park, which had been taken over by the RAF, and in the evenings he and his colleagues usually went into Manchester, either to the cinema or to the Ritz ballroom run by Mecca. They were each given a key to the house by the Jewish family living in the house and told what time the door would be bolted. One night Don got back late and only managed to get in by climbing through a window. On another evening the man of the house gave each of the lads tickets to a cinema in Manchester.

After about three weeks in the flat, going daily by tram to Heaton Park, they were told that space was now available for them there so they had to pack and were moved to a hut in the park. There was generally not much to do in the park, a certain amount of drill and a lot of sitting around. One evening a few flights, including Don's, were told they were confined to barracks for some misdemeanour, just when poor old Don had arranged to meet someone in Manchester. However, he knew that some flights would be leaving the camp and that they did this by marching out under the control of a corporal, who showed his authority at the gate and then dismissed the boys outside. He knew each flight would be halted at the gates whilst the corporal in charge showed his pass to those on the gate, he decided to go over and hide in some bushes near the gate and await the arrival of a flight. When one duly arrived and halted he let those in the rear ranks see him and made them understand he wanted to join them; they soon reshuffled and made space for him in the ranks and thus he was marched out through the gate to be dismissed outside. He kept his date.

'Careless talk costs lives' was a common sign put up everywhere but Manchester took the biscuit as so many people seemed to know of 'troop' movements. Don was told one evening by a girl in a pub that his flight would be moving out and that the *Queen Mary* was waiting up north to take them overseas. She proved right, for a day later they were taken in lorries to the station and boarded a train which went north and the following morning arrived at Gourock where they were marched to a paddle steamer which took them out into the middle of the Clyde where they boarded a big liner, the *Queen Mary*!

Don and his friends were placed on one of the lower decks and being told the ship would be nearly empty when it sailed, all RAF personnel were to be allocated jobs to do on the journey. Some were given the job of patrolling the ship to make sure there were no saboteurs, others were given police duties, some working in the kitchens and others on cleaning the decks. Don and friends were on cleaning duties and their task was to wash the main staircase from Sun deck down to E deck in the bowels of the ship. They had to report to start their duty at midnight and after completing they were free for the rest of the night and day. It was a good job to have as it only lasted about two hours, however, there was one snag for Don – he was sea sick on the first night out and the sergeant in charge had to send him back to his cabin; he managed to survive the remainder of the voyage. During the day he and his friends usually sat on deck, talked and played cards. The ship zigzagged the whole way and having had its stabilising gear removed it rolled terribly and looking sideways you saw all sky one moment and all sea the next. In later years Don learnt that the *Mary* had indeed almost capsized on one of these zigzag crossings when it was hit by a tremendous wave, in fact it was later established that one or two degrees further over and it would have capsized. The book *The Poseidon Adventure* was written based on this happening.

Whilst on the crossing, rumours persisted that the ship was being chased by the German battleship, *Tirpitz*, and of course it was known that German submarines would look upon the sinking of the *Queen Mary* as a major prize. The *Mary* must have travelled far north on this crossing as it got very cold although it was mid-August, but eventually after one or two days moving in a southerly direction an announcement was made over the tannoy that the ship would soon be entering New York harbour. It had been seven days since they had set sail from the Clyde and on the announcement there was a general rush to the upper decks to see the ship approach Manhattan. He stood next to an American soldier who said he had never been to New York before and Don, having pre war bought an atlas from Woolworths which had an aerial photograph of New York with description of buildings and places of interest, was able to point out these places as they were passed. The ship docked on the west of Manhattan right opposite the Empire State Building, then the tallest building in the world. An American Army band was playing on the quayside and fellows awaiting the order to disembark were soon leaning out of portholes and over railings shouting out what they hoped the band would play, particularly 'In the mood', which the band eventually played. When Don's party disembarked they were met by many ladies handing out magazines, chocolates etc., and after a short while his flight was told to form up but instead of marching towards Manhattan they were marched to the other end of the pier where they boarded a boat that took them across the Hudson River to Jersey City where they boarded a waiting train. So they were not to see New York, much to the disappointment of all, and instead were taken north out of the built-up area and into the country along the side of the Hudson River. Soon the train passed a station with the name Sing Sing which brought back memories to Don of certain American gangster prison films and now he knew why in many films when instead of saying a man had gone to prison they said he had gone up the river.

The journey north continued and late in the afternoon the conductor came round to show how beds were brought down from above the seats with the seats themselves being converted to beds making the whole carriage a sleeping car, black curtains forming a corridor down the middle.

It was understood that during the night the train had crossed into Canada then back into the state of Maine and finally back into Canada calling at St John, the capital of the province of New Brunswick, and not long after arrived at Moncton which the RAF boys had been told was their destination.

It was nine o'clock in the morning when the train pulled into Moncton and soon the RAF boys had disembarked and were piled into lorries with their kit bags and were driven the short distance to the nearby RAF transit camp. Don and the rest of the flight were directed to one of the many two-storey white huts which would be their home until a further posting arrived. There seemed to be scores of aircrew on the station waiting for postings, some back to the UK having completed their training and others like Don's flight waiting to go somewhere in Canada. Those going back to the UK were nearly all sergeants and officers, some with pilot wings, some with navigator brevets and yet others with those of air gunners.

The food on the camp was good and apart from one or two lectures and a certain amount of drill there was quite a lot of spare time for writing letters, playing cards or just talking. The evenings were free and, although there was a cinema on the camp, most lads, certainly in the early days on the camp, made their way into town for the evening. One day Don was surprised to meet a boy from his old school who he learnt was on his way back to the UK and to civilian life! It seems he had failed aircrew training through consistent airsickness and since he had, before joining the RAF, worked in a reserved occupation he would be returning to that work since the law stated that one could only leave a reserved occupation in wartime by volunteering for aircrew or submarine duties.

The flights used to parade each morning and were then generally dismissed to do what one liked within the camp. One morning the corporal in charge asked for volunteers to give blood at the local hospital and men were encouraged to do so by a rumour to the effect that they would get a 48-hour pass. Don volunteered together with a number of others and was taken by lorry to the hospital and on their return were indeed duly given the pass. As part of the 48, Don and two friends took a train to a nearby seaside but the weather was not good and the place dead, so they soon came back.

A few weeks passed before a posting for him and his friends arrived and the following morning they were taken by lorry to the rail station where they boarded a train going west.

Once again they were in carriages which could be converted at night into sleeping cars and they learnt they would be using these sleeping arrangements for the next several nights. The train kept a slow steady speed with hardly a change in the monotonous rhythm of the wheels which was so different from that of trains at that time in England. Don learnt that the different rhythm was caused by the welding of the rails which British railways had not then carried out. The train stopped several times and at one or two long stops of a half an hour or so; passengers were allowed to leave the train and visit nearby shops. Some days into the journey, whilst the train was riding north of the Great Lakes, the conductor pointed out an Indian Reservation and at the next stop, Sioux Lookout, there were many Red Indians selling their wares to the passengers.

The following morning the train left the country of forests and lakes and rode onto the prairie and was soon passing big grain elevators close by rail stations. Soon they were going through a built-up area by marshalling yards and then into a big station below ground, Winnipeg, where the train stopped. Don and friends were ordered to leave the train and form up in threes on the platform, then a sergeant marched them forward and up a slope to the ground level of the station. As they started up the slope they could see faces peering over the top and "Here they come" was heard several times. The unsuspecting airmen lifted their chests and began to march with more purpose and, as they broke clear at the top, the crowds of people were cheering and clapping and they heard, "Here's the boys – aren't they young!" The flight halted and then dismissed and all were soon surrounded by the waiting people who had taken time to come and meet the train bringing airmen from the Old Country. "Where do you come from?" "Oh my Pa came from there", "Any time you are in Winnipeg do look us up", "What is it like now back home?" etc. Don and the boys were quite overwhelmed by the welcome and the utter surprise made it all the more pleasant.

However, it was not to last as they were told they would not be staying and would shortly be boarding another train to take them to a place called Neepawa which they learnt was about 120 miles distance. The boys soon were called to form up and marched off below to where the train was waiting. A few hours later they were driven in trucks to the airfield about a mile or so out of town.

Chapter Twenty-Two

Neepawa was an RAF station but most of the ground crew were civilians living in the town. The planes used were Tiger Moths, the same as Don had flown in England but there was a difference – these aircraft had canopies over the two seats which were obviously put there so that flying could continue in the cold Canadian winter. Winnipeg and Neepawa are in the province of Manitoba which is right in the centre of the land mass of Canada and being furthest away from the oceans was the coldest prairie province in winter and yet the hottest in the summer.

The town was quite small, and reminded Don of western towns he had seen in cowboy films. None of the roads out of town were tarmacadamed although they were substantial and well graded on the very occasional bends.

His time in Neepawa passed quite quickly as they were kept very busy on both ground work and flying. Don's instructor gave him a few hours' flying before he sent him off solo and on this first flight he had quite an adventure. He dropped the instructor on the apron and taxied towards the take-off point, as he did so he was waved back by the pilot of a passing Tiger going the opposite way which made Don think there was something wrong with his plane and so he taxied back and asked one of the ground crew to check around the plane. He said everything was fine so back went Don, did his cockpit check, opened the throttle and was tearing across the field when a red flare was shot from the control tower – too late! The plane shot through cloud and he found he was above a sea of cloud with not a break anywhere to be seen. He of course now realised why the pilot in the other Tiger had waved him back and why the control tower had shot a red flare. He was on his own up there and not any ground in sight. He looked around the sky and in the distance saw another Tiger and feeling sure that the pilot of that plane would know more than him what to do, he opened his throttle and made to catch him up and follow. He gained on him but suddenly the other plane flew down into the cloud, so Don followed and almost at once was through the thin cloud layer and flying close to the ground about a half a mile behind the other Tiger. He followed and very soon saw what must be the airfield perimeter fence and hopping over this ran into land and taxied back. No harm done – he had been lucky!

Some of the flying was carried out at night and one instructor, who Don thought must have been a little nervous, was not happy with one of Don's take-offs saying he nearly stalled the aircraft. He duly reported Don to the senior instructor who immediately took him up for a test flight. Everything went well and Don passed. However, the 'nervous instructor' never flew with him again.

On free evenings most of the lads either went to the station cinema or into town, where there was not of course much to do except go to the town cinema, or the occasional dance, or what appealed to Don most, go to a café and buy a T-bone steak with French fries, price one dollar. There were also a few 48s with most opting to go to Winnipeg where Don and two friends found a good bed and breakfast – the lady of the house was always pleased to see them, especially Red, as she always called Don, a name he liked better than Ginger.

Travelling to Winnipeg on most 48s was by train but there was one occasion when Don and a friend decided they would try hitch-hiking in order to save money. They caught the bus into Neepawa after flying finished for the day and straightway set off walking on the road to Portage la Prairie where they knew they would pick up the trans Canada highway which would take them to Winnipeg. There was not much traffic but the first car going their way pulled up when they signalled and they were lucky as the driver said he was going all the way down to Portage.

It was dark when they arrived in Portage and they decided to find a bed and breakfast for the night. They bought a drink in a saloon and started talking to the man behind the bar. He said he had a room they could stay in for the night and then proceeded to give them tickets for the local cinema which he said he owned. They went to the cinema, spent the night in the room he provided, had breakfast and the man would not take any money. They of course thanked him and started off east down the trans Canada highway.

They had not gone far when the sky started getting very black and a few snowflakes fell. They continued on but not one car passed them going east. Soon the snow got heavier and a short while later it was snowing so hard that it was difficult to see more than a yard or two in front. It was also getting deep underfoot and they decided to turn around and go back whence they had come. They now could not see any of the telegraph poles so they were not sure in which direction they were going. However, they pressed on believing they would soon reach Portage as they knew they had not walked far on the road before it snowed. After fifteen minutes or so there was still no trace of Portage and they then began to realise they were lost, it was difficult to walk or to speak to each other as the wind was so strong. They pressed on for another fifteen minutes or so when quite suddenly they came up against an obstruction which they soon realised was a wooden building, perhaps a shed. If it were a shed then it must have a door, so they felt their way round, found the door, but it was locked. However, on this side it was more sheltered and they thought they must stay there before wandering off further into the black. They had only been there a minute or two when they heard a dog bark and then through the darkness saw a light and very soon a man carrying a torch. He beckoned them to follow and led them with the dog to some steps to a door which he opened and told them to follow. It was only then that they realised their rescuer was a Red Indian and he had taken them to his log cabin where inside was his wife working on a wooden table in the centre of a square room with a big fire burning in the grate close by. He told them to take off their wet coats and hung them near the fire whilst his wife offered them a mug of steaming liquid which was tea without milk. At the end of the room there was a low gallery and peeping through the balustrade were two small children, obviously curious to see who their father had brought into the house.

Don and friend thanked their host for looking after them and explained what had happened. It seemed they must have wandered a good way off the main road and were lucky to have bumped into the shed or else they might have wandered further away from the road and into the deep country. The Indian told them that he owned the log cabin and the land around which in the summer he farmed. He said he had left a reservation in Saskatchewan some five years before.

It was about an hour later when the snow quite suddenly stopped and very soon the sun was shining and it was possible to see the road as a snow plough passed shooting snow into the air and into the fields. The road must have been nearly half a mile away. Soon one or two cars were seen on the road and Don said they would like to get back on the road, so their host, carrying a shovel, guided them back to the road and dug a path through the piles of snow by the roadside to enable them to stand on the now cleared highway. They thanked him warmly and started walking east. The next car that came along stopped and the driver said he was going all the way to Winnipeg and thus took them along, right up to the bed and breakfast house where they were going to stay and where they met up with other friends who had travelled to Winnipeg by train.

That night in a bar in the city centre, Don was surprised to meet an old friend from school. Migs Morgan had just passed out as a navigator and was on his way back to England, and as he said, to marry a girl who Don knew well and who a few years before he had taken to the cinema. Later Don was to discover that Migs had married her but sadly not long afterwards had been killed whilst on a raid over Germany.

The Neepawa course finished and he passed, but sadly had earlier lost one or two of his best friends washed out and sent onto a navigator course. Just before Christmas his intake were given a posting to a station in Saskatchewan which meant a long and tedious journey by train, changing more than once. They arrived early one morning at Estevan, and on leaving the train station he was again reminded of cowboy films, very much more so than Neepawa, as the town resembled one of the towns featured in so many westerns, much more so than any other town he had seen in Canada The airfield, out of town, was again an RAF station and having just settled in they were told on the next day that a mistake had been made in sending them there as the station was due to close and the last course had already started. They were told they would have to wait for another posting and in the meantime were going to be given jobs to do on the station. One of the first they were given was to polish the floor of the hut in which they were housed and it was whilst polishing, by pulling a small chap on a blanket along the hut, that an airmen entered and shouted out for LAC Moggs to report to the Station Warrant Officer. Don of course wondered what it was all about but went with the messenger to the SWO's office, knocked, went in, stood to attention, gave his name and his last three[2] and waited for the man seated in front of him to speak.

Much to his surprise the man said, "Where do you come from, lad?"

"A town called Enfield, in Middlesex, Sir."

"What was your father's name?"

"Bert."

---

[2] In the RAF you are given a number, six or seven digits long, and when giving your name you also give the last three digits of your number.

"I wondered when I saw the name, I had never met anyone else with that name. I too am from Enfield and I knew your dad, went to school with him and met him again in France during the last war."

There followed a brief conversation when the SWO finally said, "Your dad was a good sort, I'll look after you, lad, whilst you are here."

And he did, Don and one or two of his friends were the following day given easy jobs to do on the orders of this SWO who they understood could be a right bastard. However, the light work did not last very long as it was decided that since no posting was imminent and Christmas upon them, they would all be given 14 days' leave. But where to go when you are miles from anywhere was the question. However, Don had a friend in the flight near to his own age who, although a Canadian, had joined the RAF having pre joining lived in Los Angeles, working for Technicolor. Bart had on a number of occasions shown the boys pictures of some of the girls, including film stars he had known and it was not surprising that he said he was going down to LA and said he might be able to fix it for some others to come along too. It was necessary, they had been told, to have an invitation before one was allowed to cross over into the USA. Don and friends, keen to go, went into town with Bart to a telephone booth by the rail station so that he could ring his aunt who he would ask for an invitation.

All the lads crowded inside the telephone booth as Bart turned the handle to get the attention of the operator. "I want to make a call to Los Angeles, California." Bart did not seem to get an answer and afterwards said that there was a stunned silence before the operator asked him to repeat, which he did and said he wanted to make the call collect, or as one would say in England 'reversed charges', if that were possible. He gave the operator the name of the person to whom he wished to speak and her telephone number, he was told to put the receiver down and that the operator would ring back when the call was through. One could imagine the panic there must have been

114

when the operator was asked to get LA as the lads were sure such a call had never been asked for before. The lads speculated that before putting the call through the operator would be ringing around the town telling people what she was about to do. Anyway about ten minutes later the call came through and Bart answered; he talked to his aunt and explained what he wanted and gave the names of the people he wanted invited, the lads pushing forward to make sure their name was put on the list, but from the shouting Bart was having to resort to it was clear the line was bad as he had to keep repeating names and spelling them out – he afterwards confirmed this.

The days passed and no telegram, the leave was due to start the next day and Don and the others had to make a decision. It seemed it was just not going to happen so they went into Estevan and bought tickets on the train for Winnipeg leaving early the following morning. However, the next morning, just as they were about to leave the camp for the rail station, the telegram arrived but the only name showing clearly was that of Don Moggs. The others were just not legible and they knew it was unlikely any border guard would accept, and in any event they had just spent a lot of money buying tickets for Winnipeg, so they reluctantly decided that was where they would go.

In Winnipeg they went to the usual bed and breakfast and the following morning, Christmas Day, went along to the Airmen's Club in town. The place was almost deserted, only a few Canadian airmen and Don and his two friends were there. They bought a drink and started to play on the empty snooker table. Outside the streets were empty and the weather very cold and uninviting. They had been playing about half an hour when a man came into the club and asked if there were any English boys around. He said he was a taxi driver and wanted two English boys to take to a family out of Winnipeg for Christmas dinner. Don said, "There are three of us and we are not splitting up."

The driver looked pensive for a moment and then, "Oh what the hell! All three of you come along, I'm sure they won't mind an extra one."

So they were driven to a small town called Stonewall, just over twenty miles outside Winnipeg. The husband and his wife were originally from England and they were told that most of this town's inhabitants had English connections. The boys were given dinner and asked to stay overnight. The man of the house was the town mayor and the following day he took the boys to meet various people in the town, introduced them to the skating rink, and showed them the snow-covered golf course. That evening they were entertained by the next-door neighbour, a Dr Evelyn, who claimed to be a direct descendant of the English diarist.

The house in which they stayed was centrally heated by a wood-fired boiler in the basement which sent warm air through ducts to each room. This was of course the first time Don had been in a house with central heating and knew of none in England, but understood why it was needed out there when temperatures could reach 40 below. Later that day the boys were happy to chop piles of wood for storage in the basement; enough to carry the household through to the end of the winter.

Although they enjoyed their stay with the family and particularly being introduced and playing curling on the town rink, they still wanted to get back to Winnipeg where there was much more to do. The family tried to get them to stay longer but the pull of the bright lights was too great. Back in Winnipeg Don met a young lady at a dance collecting for a charity and who was being pestered by men as she went around the dance hall, Don offered himself as minder and helped her that evening. The following day she took him skating on the Red River. This was the second river he had skated on since coming to Canada as he had several times before skated at Neepawa on the Whitemud river, although Red River was much wider and being covered with snow worried him a bit

116

that there might be an unseen break in the ice, he was assured however that the ice was several inches thick all over.

The leave ended and they returned to Estevan and a day or so later were sent on their way to their next posting which was to an RCAF station up north in Manitoba, a town called Dauphin. They arrived in Dauphin after a very tiring journey of over twenty-four hours and had hardly set foot on the station when they were taken out to the airport's relief drome, some five miles out of town, as there was insufficient accommodation for them on the main airport.

Chapter Twenty-Three

Dauphin was a Service Flying Training School (SFTS), as indeed had been Estevan, but this new station was Canadian and Don's intake was, they were told, the first RAF one to be trained on that station. The first impressions were not good, for not only was it rumoured the Canadians did not like them or want them on their station but as there was now such a surplus of aircrew trainees the fail rate would be at least fifty per cent. The relief drome was five miles out of town and there was no public transport so Don and friends were going to be kicking their heels on this way-out station until they could be moved to the main airfield, which they were informed would be at least two weeks. Don's letters home told how fed up they all were and whereas many of the lads had been keen to get on ops some were now thinking of asking for a transfer out of the RAF.

However, eventually they were found accommodation on the main station and the course began.

The station in appearance was not unlike those built in Canada for the RAF but there were a number of things different. For one it was necessary to salute the flag each time you passed it, and then there was an outdoor skating rink and indoors a bowling alley, whilst the canteen sold lots of ice cream, which pleased Don. All the instructors were Canadian and contrary to what they had been told to expect he found them to be quite friendly, in fact they had not been on the station long when the flight commander gave them a brief talk on Canada suggesting they might like to think about emigrating after the war ended.

The course work was very concentrated and the ill feeling of the early days, other than mixing with the instructors, soon

118

disappeared. The aeroplanes used were twin engine Cessna Cranes, or as they were known in the USA, Bobcats. After a few hours flying Don went solo and as the months went by so the flying became more interesting particularly when they had to go on cross country flights, flying to other airfields. On one solo flight to Saskatoon, about 300 miles distance, Don met the young brother of one of his school friends who was also training as a pilot in Saskatoon.

The number of hours flying was steadily increasing way beyond the number of hours men in earlier intakes in the war had before getting their wings and being posted on operations. The majority of flying was in the day but there was of course plenty of night flying, both dual and solo, and it was mostly at night that they practised the device used for finding the runway on an airfield, that is SBA (Standard Beam Approach). There was of course none of the sophisticated landing devices used by pilots today but at least this method helped a pilot find a runway. Since the Cessnas were not fitted out for SBA the plane used was the well-tried Avro Anson and it was on SBA work that Don on two separate occasions had problems. The first was whilst flying at night with an instructor when they smelt burning and Don was ordered to fly back to base where they landed safely and on inspection found a small engine fire. On the second occasion with the same instructor, this time in daylight, one of the engines really caught fire and after shutting off that engine they headed back to base, intending to land without doing the usual circle of the field. As they neared the base, flying on one engine with smoke pouring from the other, it seemed as if the whole station were out on the tarmac with the fire engine and blood wagon waiting for what might be a crash landing, However, they landed safely, but the instructor said he would not fly with Don again as he said he was a jinx.

Besides bowling, going to the cinema or occasionally skating, Don set up a dancing class with one of his friends, trying to get the RCAF women to come along and learn basic ballroom dancing; men were invited too, but of course only women turned up. Don with a Canadian WAAF (or as the RCAF called them, WDs i.e. Women's Division) soon had the girls dancing, which they seemed to enjoy. The gramophone used by the dancers was also used by a Canadian officer who one evening a week played classical records for any interested to hear and listen to him talk about them and the composers; Don thoroughly enjoyed these evenings.

Don wrote letters to Betty almost daily and she did the same. They numbered their letters as often two or three were received at a time and not always in a proper sequence. Don also wrote home to his parents and sister and they to him. One letter from home enclosed a POW letter from his old friend Del. Don's parents said that his friend had earlier been reported missing but they had not written to tell him until the letter arrived from Germany. The pencilled letter said that he had baled out over Germany with his crew and then tried to find his way home but after a few days had been captured and sent to Stalag Luft 3. – this was the camp which after the war became famous for the escape of many airmen, fifty of whom were shot on orders of Hitler. With the letter his parents included a photograph from the local paper under which it said Del had completed over sixty raids, with eleven being with a pathfinder squadron.

During the stay in Dauphin the lads were given one or two 48s and of course it was once again off to Winnipeg, 200 miles distant, nearly eight hours on an overnight milk train, or as on one weekend four of them went off to Riding Mountain National Park, relatively nearby, where they stayed in a rented log cabin and went horse riding.

Several weeks later after completing the set course and managing to survive whilst many friends were lost on wash-outs, Don and those left were looking forward to getting their wings. However, they were suddenly told the course would be extended and the reason given was that there was no shipping available to take them back to England. The course was extended by eight weeks and the instructors admitted they could not teach them any more so someone thought up new things for them to try. One was nine-plane formation flying which had not previously been done by trainees or instructors. It was soon found that this was somewhat hazardous in steep turns for airplanes with a maximum speed of not much more than 200 miles an hour, but in spite of the problems they eventually got it to a fine art.

In his eight months at Dauphin he played ice hockey for the RAF boys who formed a team to play the Aussies and New Zealanders who had since arrived on the station; his team won, mostly due to Don's Canadian friend, Bart, who had joined the RAF whilst living in Los Angeles. They were however not surprisingly thrashed by the Canadians as it seemed Canadians started to skate just about the same time as they started walking. The RAF boys also formed a station football team and played a few games against certain RAF stations in Manitoba. They flew to away games in an Anson, and Don, playing in all games, got a good write-up in the local *Dauphin Herald* for a goal he scored in one home game.

Eventually they were given the date for graduation and parties were arranged. All aircrew graduated as sergeants and it was necessary for stripes to be sewn on tunics the night before the parade. However, a few RAF and all the Canadians on the course were taken aside two days before and told they would be getting commissions, but nevertheless they had to get stripes sewn on their tunics; Don was one of those told he was to be commissioned and managed to get his dance partner to sew on the stripes.

The parade was to be outside on the square but on the morning it started to pour with rain and everything had to be transferred to one of the hangers. A number of people arrived to watch and a small stand was erected inside, mostly the guests were parents of the few Canadians they had put onto the RAF course, but there were also one or two girlfriends of RAF personnel. The presentation went smoothly with each airman after his name and where he was from being announced, marching forward to the officer presenting the wings, smartly saluting and after about turn returning to the ranks. The parade finally being marched out of the hanger with the station band playing and then when outside being dismissed. Those being granted commissions had then to go to the officers' mess where they were introduced to other officers present, all Canadians, and then were given certificates and a white arm band to wear over their stripes until they could buy their uniforms.

Don had a couple of days before, when advised of his commission, been told that he would not be going back to England as he had been chosen with four others to take a navigator's course on Prince Edward Island for eventual transfer to Coastal Command. He was of course very upset as he had planned to get married once he returned home, however, he was advised not to protest as they told him he was well thought of and it would go against his future career if he did so. He thus accepted it and wrote to tell Betty and his parents. The course would be nine weeks and would start four weeks from graduation in Dauphin. They would have the opportunity to get their uniforms in Winnipeg and then take leave reporting straight to Prince Edward Island at the end of the leave.

Don and others took the train to Winnipeg and went to be fitted for uniforms at the Hudson Bay Company and then returned to Dauphin where they packed, were issued with tickets to Summerside on PEI, and he and four others agreed they would break their journey in Montreal and go down to New York to spend their leave. Two days later they left and on their way collected and changed into their new uniforms in Winnipeg. Don had sufficient time to go out to Stonewall and see the family who had entertained him and his friends the previous Christmas. They tried to get him to stay over instead of going to New York but he had made up his mind and that evening he and the others caught the Trans Canada Express that would take them east to Montreal. They of course had to buy their own tickets down from Montreal to New York and instead of the luxury of sleeping berths they had enjoyed from

Winnipeg decided to sit up in the day coach arriving in New York the following morning.

In New York they went along to the English Speaking Union where they had been told accommodation could be arranged. There they were able to choose the type of holiday they wanted, they could stay with a family or be given an apartment and look after themselves. Don and an Argentinean friend, Derek, chose the latter and were sent to an impressive apartment off Park Avenue, the home of a shipping millionaire.

In New York they did most everything and thoroughly enjoyed their stay in the city which was so unlike wartime London. They spent little money as people wanted to treat them and the accommodation was free. The leave ended and back they went up to Montreal and then on the long journey to PEI. Prince Edward Island is the smallest Canadian Province and outside Canada is probably only known for being the setting for the well-known book *Anne of Green Gables*. On arriving back they were told the course could still not be started, so once again they were sent on leave. Most wanted to go back to New York but were told they would not be allowed across the border due to a polio scare, so they decided to go to Montreal instead. Although a very long way from PEI, and thus a costly train journey, it may seem surprising they would still have enough money to pay their fare and accommodation, which they knew would not be free as in New York, when they had just come back from a long holiday, but pay for an officer in the RCAF was very high.

They spent two weeks in Montreal but did not enjoy it nearly as much as in New York, the people were not exactly friendly, probably some being Vichy French as was demonstrated one day at the rail station where a big crowd had gathered to greet the ex-mayor who had just been freed from internment as a Vichy sympathiser, or so Don was told by a Canadian standing near to him in the crowd. Don and friends spent their time window shopping, going to the cinema and once to a football game at McGill University. They left

Montreal in time to get back to Summerside where the course began.

There was to be a lot of flying as first and second navigators and of course plenty of ground work. The flying was all carried out at low altitudes over the Gulf of St Lawrence, never more than 1500 feet which under cloud cover made the flying very bumpy. Don was often sick as first navigator whose job was to plot the course for the pilot to fly whilst the second navigator looked out for fixes. The planes used were Anson Vs and at night the second navigator when checking wind speed had to open the plane door and lying on his stomach throw out the flares by which the drift could be measured.

The GR (General Reconnaissance) course kept everyone busy and there was little free time and, in any event, nothing much to do. Some fellows went to visit Charlottetown, the island capital, but were not impressed. The nine weeks went by quite quickly and Don with the others passed out and were issued with navigators' certificates in the RCAF. Then there was more leave!

Don and friends without hesitation decided that New York would be their destination, the ban on crossing the border having been lifted. But before leaving they were all told where would be their next stop. Don and some of his friends were told they were destined for Nassau in the Bahamas but Don had his mind set on going home and asked if he could change with someone onto a home posting. The flight commander agreed and Don had no difficulty in getting someone to change postings as all seemed to want to go to the Bahamas and not home where it was said one would soon be on operations.

Don had by chance met up with an old friend from his very early days in the RAF, who had joined the course in Summerside and it was with Fred Green that he shared an apartment in New York. It was Fred's first visit there and thus he had to be shown all the high spots. The apartment allocated to them by the English Speaking Union was owned by Jean S Roosevelt who was, they were told, a niece of Theodore

Roosevelt, the president in the early 1900s. They were advised by the lady at the Union not to speak too highly of the then president of the USA, Franklin Delano Roosevelt, as he was considered to be the black sheep of the family, being a Democrat!

The apartment had a lift which opened directly into it and they were given a lovely bedroom with two single beds and having met the owner were told they would be given breakfast each day and of course two keys to the apartment.

The stay in New York was again a great success and was over too soon. Don, Fred and others visited many places of interest and in one, The Rockefeller Centre, he was asked to be interviewed on television which was shown throughout the Centre and perhaps elsewhere; television, it should be remembered, was then in its infancy. He had his leg pulled after as the others who had seen the interview said people around watching kept saying, "Oh isn't he nice." Unfortunately Fred and the others had to leave the city before him as they had to get down to the Bahamas, so Don was left on his own for the best part of a week before it was his time to catch the train up to Montreal and then on to Moncton where he was to await posting home. He was given a nice letter from Mrs Roosevelt wishing him well in his forthcoming wedding.

It was late November when he left New York and the train had not gone far when the weather turned nasty and it started to snow. Some time later the conductor advised all on board that the train was being delayed due to the snow. Don told him that he had booked a sleeping berth on the Canadian Trans Continental from Montreal and wondered if he would be there in time to get his connection. The conductor said he would get through to Montreal and speak to them. Later he came back to say that Don should get off the train at Lachine Junction before Montreal and there the Trans Continental would stop to pick him up. They got to Lachine and thanking the conductor was directed to wait for his train from Montreal. He had been there only a short time when in came the mighty engine pulling some sixteen or eighteen coaches and stopped. A conductor appeared from one of the doors and called him over. He boarded and was shown to his berth. The Trans Continental Express had stopped just to pick him up! It was hard to believe, but it happened.

The following morning he was once more back in Moncton to await posting back to the UK. He had arranged with Betty that they would get married on his disembarkation leave but first he had to get RAF approval and thus he went to the Chaplain who issued an appropriate note of approval.

Now almost eighteen months since he left England and waiting in Moncton for a posting home it is probably a good time to let the reader know that although much of what has been written before may sound a series of enjoyable adventures, which many were, he and all the others were nevertheless well aware the end would almost certainly be operations against the enemy. As is now known, RAF Bomber Command alone lost nearly 55,000 aircrew killed and life expectancy of aircrew generally was not great. Training for aircrew was of course not without casualties and Don well remembered being one of a firing party at a funeral of a victim of a crash and later was to hear that his Argentinean friend Derek with whom he had spent two weeks with in New York had died in the Bahamas when two Liberator aircraft collided in the air. Then after the war he was to learn that the England fast bowler, Kenneth Farnes, mentioned earlier in the story, who as a schoolboy he had gone to see at Lords, was killed when training as a pilot. No, the 'fun' was soon expected to be over.

Don, in giving up his posting to the Bahamas, knew very well that he would most likely be on operations before the Bahama boys, but he wanted to see Betty who he had missed terribly while away, even though he had often found comfort with other girls away from home. He knew she too had seen other men, and who could blame her, a town girl living the war years in a Bedfordshire country village surrounded by

126

American and RAF personnel with the evacuated girls frequently being invited to stations for dances.

Chapter Twenty-Four

A week or so later and the posting arrived and he was once more on a train, this time to Halifax. It was now one week before Christmas and the captain of the ship they boarded, the new *Mauretania*, said he would do his best to get the boys back for Christmas – and he almost succeeded, but not quite. The ship arrived outside the Mersey on Christmas Eve but could not enter due to fog and was not allowed in to dock until Christmas Day. All on board had been given an excellent Christmas dinner the day before but were now stuck on board as there were no dockers to unload the ship and get baggage from the hold. Instead of getting off, everyone was held on board and issued with American K rations. They were all glad to be back in England but disappointed at not being allowed off the ship. The day after Boxing Day they were disembarked and Don and others reported to Harrogate, a holding centre for aircrew.

He telephoned his fiancée at her place of work and told her he should be coming home in a few days but first had a certain routine to go through before he could leave. Betty had already made preparations for the wedding with the local church and said she would now fix it for 3rd January. Don meanwhile read a notice that all officers intending to marry on disembarkation leave were to report to the station adjutant. The call to the adjutant's office was to show the chaplain's approval obtained in Canada but mostly, Don saw afterwards, was so that the adjutant could sell insurance, he particularly emphasising that the next posting would almost certainly be to the Far East where he claimed more died from tropical disease than from war and therefore it was wise to get insurance, which of course he happened to sell. The fact that Don later found the policy he took out did not cover tropical disease is another story.

On the day before leaving he again telephoned Betty and told her the time he would be arriving at Kings Cross station and on arriving he was met, not just by Betty, but by his mother and father also. He soon grasped that the wedding having been arranged for January 3rd and thus giving little time for things to be prepared, had not been too well received by his parents and he straightaway sensed this and the atmosphere was unfortunately tense.

On the evening before the wedding he pressed his uniform at home and hung it on a picture rail to air in the room where there had been a coal fire during the day. The following morning Don and his mother and sister had just finished breakfast in the front room of the house and were now in the scullery at the back, the ladies washing up and Don polishing his shoes for the wedding when suddenly everything went black with sparks flying everywhere, followed immediately by a tremendous noise and the ladies grabbed hold of Don screaming. When he saw they were unhurt and of course realising they had been bombed, he rushed to the front of the house and outside. He did not have to open the front door as it had gone. Outside it was deathly quite except for some crying and a lady's voice calling from a house on the opposite side of the road. He ran over to the house and rushed inside; there was no door, and up the stairs passing bare electrical wiring sparking away. A lady was calling from what proved to be the bathroom, he tried the door but it was jammed, the lady was calling out for her baby. He rushed into one of the bedrooms from where he could hear crying and found a little girl sitting in the middle of a bed with everything around her and herself covered in ceiling plaster and dirt. The tears on her face were wiping the dirt from her face. Don grabbed her, told the mother she was all right and said he would come back. He ran down the stairs and passing two men on their way up, quickly told them where the mother was and continued down the stairs and carried the little girl over to his parents' home. By this time the street was alive with people and shortly ambulances and fire engines arrived. He looked into the room where he had hung his uniform and lo and behold it was still there in spite of the tablecloth and what remained on the breakfast table having all disappeared out with the window. The uniform, RAF officer blue, was now grey with plaster dust. An hour or so later one of Betty's brothers, who lived at home about a mile and a half away, came round on his bicycle to find out what had happened and indeed whether there was going to be a wedding. Generally people did not have telephones in their houses but news travelled quickly and Betty's family, having heard the explosion and seeing the smoke, knew almost for certain that a V2 rocket had fallen somewhere near to where Don lived. In fact the rocket had fallen directly opposite his parents' house not more than 30 yards from the front of the house. Most of the roof and all the front windows had been blown out from their home and of course many other houses in the road had also been badly damaged. Among all the mayhem, the best man arrived on the train from Enfield, again having heard that a bomb had fallen near to Bush Hill Park railway station and thus next to where he knew Don lived.

Don eventually went with his best man back to his house in order to clean his uniform and then straight on to the church where the wedding was to take place.

Some of Don's Air Force friends turned up as they had promised but his parents did not attend, only his sister coming along. Betty had arranged for a short honeymoon in Colwyn Bay, North Wales, and had also booked an hotel in London for the wedding night before travelling to Wales the next day. They cancelled the honeymoon but decided to take the one night in the hotel. It was a bad mistake, as London was under a V weapon attack all night, and the sound of explosions and the noise of fire engines, ambulances and police cars went on all through the night. The next morning Don and his bride returned to north London and over the next week they helped to clear up at his home. A kind aunt of Betty's purposely went to stay with a friend so that the young couple could have the use of her flat during the leave period. He managed to get a week's compassionate extension to the leave by ringing Air Ministry in London and did the same for a WAAF who lived nearby and whose house had also been damaged.

It was this week's extension that changed things for him and after the war he always claimed it could have helped save his life. He returned to Harrogate at the leave end only to find all the fellows he had come over with from Canada had already been posted to an OTU (Operational Training Unit) and he was now on his own. He was eventually sent on a posting to a small airfield near Hatfield, a pre-war flying school called Panshanger. He was billeted with others in a large house between Hatfield and St Albans and was taken in to the airfield each day in a lorry. Here they flew Tiger Moths and waited. It was while here that one morning he decided with his companion in the flight to find the mansion where Betty worked. It did not take long to find Luton and then fly north following the road to Bedford and they were soon over Wrest Park. Don dived down and flying low along the long drive flew past the front of the mansion. Several people out walking waved up at the plane – at this time in the war they would have been certain it was not an enemy plane, but unfortunately Betty did not see the display; she did afterwards say she heard the noise!

A few days later he was given a posting and was told he would be going out East. He was told to report to Blackpool after a few more days' leave. Here he was placed with others in a small hotel from where they had to report for inoculations and to collect khaki drill uniforms. Having learnt they could be there for a while, that is until a ship were ready to take them overseas, Don arranged for Betty to come up to Blackpool to stay until he had to go. They spent a few days together and then he was told one day that he and the others waiting there had to be at Blackpool station at three the following morning. The lads sleeping in another small hotel nearby threw stones up to Don's bedroom window to make sure he got down on time.

131

Chapter Twenty-Five

The train left Blackpool and eventually arrived several hours later at Gourock where they were taken out to a ship at anchor in the middle of the river surrounded by many other ships. The ship was an old steamer called the *Cameronia* and they were stuck on board for week before it finally sailed in convoy. On the first morning when going on deck after they set sail, he was surprised to see the ship sailing close by on the port side was the very ship he had sailed in on the school cruise in 1936. It was HM Troopship *Dilwara* and it sailed alongside for a whole week until they reached Gibraltar when the convoy broke up and Don's ship sailed unescorted into the Mediterranean. The ship carried on without escort until it picked up a destroyer while passing Crete, which was still occupied by the Germans. After a week sailing along the Med they arrived at Port Said where they disembarked and were sent to a tented camp on sand close to the Suez Canal. They stayed under canvas for a few nights, being waited on by Italian prisoners of war, and then were trained down the canal to a place called El Cantara where they crossed over the canal and boarded another train which took them over the Sinai desert into Palestine, then a British Mandate. They left the train at Lydda and were taken by lorries up to Jerusalem and settled in a building known as the Italian hospital.

Jerusalem was the aircrew reception centre for the Middle East and for Don and his friends there was nothing to do but wait for a posting. He had been crewed up with a bunch of boys he had come out with from Hatfield and who had trained on flying boats at the American Navy base at Pensacola in Florida. However, instead of Sunderland Flying Boats, rumours persisted that the posting would be to Nicosia in Cyprus to fly

Beaufighters, destined for Japanese shipping strikes. Meanwhile Don and friends went sightseeing and of course the most interesting was the Old City of Jerusalem as distinct from the modern city occupied mainly by Jews. The nearest entrance to the Old City was through the Jaffa gate and they went through this several times and wandered round the narrow alleyways which did not look as if they had been changed since biblical times. Every so often whilst out and about in the town one would see small columns of Jewish boys marching in twos, all in step, and kept in time by short blasts on a whistle, obviously in training for something. There had at this time been rumours of Jews going to start trouble now the war in Europe was nearing its end, and this was confirmed when a Jewish girl he met offered to take him along to an underground meeting that she attended. Don asked her what she thought all the RAF pilots were doing in Jerusalem, and suggested that if the Jews started any trouble the aircrew there would flatten Tel Aviv. Little did he know then that a year later, after he and others had left Jerusalem, that the Jews would indeed rise up and cause trouble which eventually led to the birth of the country called Israel.

Up until then Don had not been to Tel Aviv but a week or so later he was given seven days' leave and decided to take the bus down to the coast and see this Jewish City. He stayed in the officers' club with two or three other friends. The club was situated on the sea front, right next to the beach, and there he met a South African Army officer with whom he became friendly and who showed him around the town, all very modern and clean. He also met a young lady whilst there who showed him a few places of interest outside the town. One night seeing the girl back to her home, which he learnt was the other side of the adjoining town, Jaffa, he was surprised that the taxi driver spoke with a Jewish cockney accent, the man told him he had been a taxi driver in London before the war.

In order to keep the RAF aircrew occupied the officer commanding in Jerusalem thought it would be a good idea to organise a 'war game', in which every fit man was to take part. Half would 'defend the town' and the others would be taken out of town in enclosed lorries, so there was no chance of seeing where one was going, and then find their own way back and try to get past the other men left behind, who were told to take up positions around the town. Don was in the convoy of lorries to be taken out of town and when they arrived at their destination they found themselves dumped on high ground without a building in sight. They did not know whether they were north or south of the city but reasoned it was probably north. They then split into two groups, Don's group setting off down the valley, the others set off keeping on high ground so they could more easily see habitation.

After walking for several miles someone in his group said he was sure he had seen smoke ahead in the valley, and there it was in the distance and coming towards them. Assuming the railway line must be somewhere further along the valley they set off at a good pace and sure enough there was the line and just a short way ahead a country station. There were only one or two Arabs at the station and the train now nearing the station slowed and stopped just as his bunch of officers arrived and who immediately started to scramble on board the rickety old carriages ignoring the loud protestations of the guard and another official, who were obviously lost as to what to do with this hoard of RAF officers invading their train without tickets. The train was apparently going to Jerusalem and as soon as it entered habitation and started rattling over points close to where it was clear the station would be, the men began jumping off, making their way to a nearby road. They were soon back at the hospital unchallenged and found that most of the defenders had not taken their task seriously and after waiting an hour or so had decided to go back. Well it was a way to spend an afternoon and in retrospect had been enjoyed by Don and his friends.

The news on the war in Europe was good and very soon Germany surrendered and they were told on the wireless and in the papers that it was to be VE Day. Drinks in the Officers' Mess were declared free and one can imagine what happened, particularly as there was very little beer and most drinks were of the short variety. There were high jinks that evening in the mess and one officer did a trick on a cane chair by sitting on it and turning a somersault backwards and landing on his feet. Don was sure he could do it too and duly went out into the middle to jeers and cheers from the onlookers, sat down, flung himself backwards and landed on his head to roars of laughter. He immediately had a big bruise rise on his forehead as the floors in the hospital, as in most buildings in the Middle East, were all stone. However, such was his state that it did not stop him from going with his friends into town to join the general merriment where there were hundreds of Army and RAF personnel making a noise in Zion Square. His party ended up in the YMCA and although he did not remember the incident, his mother told him after the war that a friend who was with him at the time and lived near his home and knew his mother, said he had nearly been knifed by an Arab who took exception to him talking to his girl. His friend told his mother that they had had to drag Don away from fighting with the Arab.

Not long after VE day he became ill and was sent to sick quarters and it was whilst he was still in hospital that the posting to Cyprus came through and all his friends came in to see him before they left. Again through no fault of his own he was alone wondering where they would send him next. A few days later he was directed to go down to Egypt on a posting to a place called Kas Fereet. This was an RAF station right by the canal opposite to Ismalia. It was pretty much a dump and he and one or two other officers were told they would shortly be posted; but where to nobody seemed to know. After a week or so they were told to take the train to Port Said, still not knowing where they were going. "Look which way the boat is pointing," they were told. They were sure it would be east. However, on arrival and directed to the ship in the dock they did not even have to look which way it was pointing, as leaning over the rails on board were hundreds of bronzed soldiers wearing the hats of men who had been serving in India or the Far East, the ship was almost certainly going back to England. As the few RAF officers climbed the gangplank to board there were of course jeers from the Army personnel already on board. The ship was apparently crowded and bunks had been built in the hold for Army officers and it was here that Don and the other RAF joined them. The bunks were all across the floor of the hold and also built up the sides. In spite of the jeers when they boarded the ship they soon found that all the Army officers were very friendly and made them welcome.

The ship was named the *Carthage* and later that evening they sailed. The captain made the whole voyage as near to a cruise as he could. The food, as on most ships, was excellent and during the day one could lie on deck sun bathing or play cards and in the evening there was a cinema and on one or two nights concerts put on by the Army. In later years Don was reminded of these when he watched the TV show *It Ain't Half Hot Mum*. Also the ship's captain when passing along the coast of Tunisia pointed out the ruins of Carthage after which the ship had been named.

The ship called into Algiers en route and after one week since leaving Port Said she anchored off Gibraltar, where there was a good deal of bartering over the ship's side, mostly with cigarettes as currency, before setting sail once more. Towards the end of the second week the ship entered the Clyde at a time when many passengers, including Don, were down below having a lunch of steak and chips. The Captain then announced that the ship would soon be passing HMS *Vanguard*, the pride of the Royal Navy, and at this announcement there was a general rush from the mess to get on deck, but Don eating his first steak since leaving Canada was determined to continue enjoying it, and with a few other hungry men stayed below. He ended up eating three steaks and never did see the battleship.

Chapter Twenty-Six

They duly docked in Glasgow and went by train to Harrogate and to the Queens Hotel as before. He surprised Betty when he rang her at work to tell her he was back in England. Don and friends were given the customary disembarkation leave and he was able to take their belated honeymoon. They stayed a week in a small hotel/boarding house in Dawlish, recommended to him by his old friend, Varnier, who had employed him as doorkeeper/bouncer, and who had seen Don's flight give a gymnastic display whilst there on holiday two years before. Don had booked first-class seats going down to Dawlish but nevertheless ended up sitting on cases in the corridor all the way down to Exeter, the train was packed, such was the state of railways at that time.

Back at Harrogate for a few days and he was then sent on a battle course with the RAF Regiment at Credenhill station, Hereford. The arduous course lasted a month and there was plenty of variety – assault courses in full pack and rifles, building bridges and derricks, the rifle range and simulated battles with long route marches. Don was of course very fit in those days and did most things well, but he did get a sergeant a little upset when whilst coming through a pipe in a stream under a bridge he accidentally dropped his rifle in the water and came through at the other end with water pouring from the barrel, the sergeant standing on the bank doing his nut!

During his month in Hereford he did manage to get home two weekends, travelling on the Saturday morning by GWR (Great Western Railway) to Paddington and, since there was not a suitable train from Paddington on Sunday evening, returning the long way round on the LMS (London Midland and Scottish Railway) from Euston to Crewe where one changed to a GWR train going south to Hereford, arriving in Hereford and back at the camp for breakfast. Both trains were always packed, particularly the one coming south from Manchester and on boarding at two in the morning one had to squeeze into the corridor and climb over sleeping service personnel huddled together on the floor and of course suffer their abuse at waking them up. Don was to go through the same procedure some months later when he once again found himself at Hereford. What one did to get home for a few hours!

Nearing the end of the battle course, he and an air-gunner friend he had made there, were supposed to make their way to a tented camp some miles distance without being 'captured' by the enemy, having crossed several fields and sampled beer in a couple of village pubs they should have passed en route, they were walking down an empty country lane with thick forests on either side when they saw a cyclist in the distance coming towards them. They decided to surprise the cyclist by firing a blank when he was near. They jumped into cover of trees by the side of the road and waited. When the cyclist was passing they fired a round, the man nearly fell off his bicycle and dismounted and looked around, Don and his friend stayed hidden but to Don's surprise he recognised the man – it was his French teacher at the school he had left in 1937. He regretted afterwards not making himself known but at the time was too ashamed to do so; he guessed the man must have been on a cycling holiday.

At the end of the course they were given a spot of leave and as they were in their hut packing to leave the station an announcement was made on a small wireless owned by one of the lads that the Americans had dropped a bomb on Japan which had caused terrible devastation – it was called an atom bomb. It was all new to those present but from the announcement it seemed they expected the war with Japan might soon come to an end. It is difficult to imagine the thoughts running through everyone's mind, for although it had been obvious the war against Japan had been going well with the Americans capturing Okinawa, relatively close to the Japanese mainland, and the British and Empire troops pushing the Japanese out of Burma, nevertheless it was still thought to be years before the fighting would end.

The following day Don went home, which was now two rooms at the top of his mother-in-law's house, and with Betty still evacuated and not back until the weekend, Don went to see his parents and his old place of work in Tottenham. Then after another atom bomb had been dropped on another Japanese city the war was over and time to celebrate. Living in North London it was easy for him to get up to the West End and join in the celebrations as he had done a few months earlier in Jerusalem. He spent a few days with Betty and then returned to Harrogate from where he was posted to Market Harborough where he and his colleagues were kept occupied by lectures and interviews on what to do after the war. There were of course marches and time spent with the RAF Regiment but having recently been with them at Credenhill he and one or two others were often excused. There were cross country runs and plenty of football at a high standard and very soon Don was playing for the station team which boasted several professionals and played two or three times a week, probably because those in command did not know what to do with everyone, there were over a thousand on camp. Don was barracked good humouredly when playing away at Husbands Bosworth as several of fellows he knew in the Middle East were on the touch line, "Send Moggs back to Jerusalem," they cried. Later Don was to be posted to that station but not before he had been held back from an earlier posting because of playing for the station team.

The wireless announced a speeding up of demobilisation but even so Don's age group it seemed was unlikely to be released for about two years. It was however, a pretty easy life but he wanted to get back to work and he knew that in order to advance in his employment he would have to start studying, so he signed up for a correspondence course with Bennett's

College in Sheffield with which he carried on until he left the services.

From Market Harborough he was posted, as mentioned above, early in 1946, to another holding station at Husbands Bosworth and here he and his colleagues were advised that they were all to be grounded, that is no more flying, and as such they would have to be given other work. Aircrew NCOs not on flying duties were to be reduced to the rank of LAC, which seemed most unfair, whilst those with commissions, such as Don, were posted to Pembrey in South Wales and given a choice of courses on which to be retrained. He chose an Accountancy and Administration course. However, whilst awaiting a place on a course there were lectures to attend, some battle training and again football. Don was picked for the station team which played local Welsh village mining teams in the area. He felt sorry for one village mining team whom they beat as the people had entertained them so well.

The school of Accountancy and Administration was set up at the same Hereford station of Credenhill and once again at weekends he had the long trek back via Crewe on Sunday nights. The course was very comprehensive and lasted nine weeks and after passing out he was first posted to a station on the Isle of Sheppey which turned out to be an Air Ministry error and then sent as Assistant Accountant officer to a station just over the North Wales border at a place called Harwarden, just a few miles from Chester. He was given the rank of Flight Lieutenant and learnt that the Senior Accountant was due to be demobbed very soon and that he was destined to take over with the rank of Squadron Leader. However, it never happened as after several weeks working there he was again posted, this time to a station in Bristol which was almost immediately cancelled, and then to a drome in Northamptonshire. He had enjoyed his stay at Harwarden, particularly being taken into Chester to collect money for payday and the occasional trips into the Wirral to pay the few men stationed at a country house called Hooton Hall. Only there a few months, nevertheless, he had obviously become quite popular as before leaving he was given a party at a local pub which all Pay Accounts and Store Account members attended.

The Northamptonshire station, Polebrook, was situated near the village of that name and had recently been taken over from the American Eighth Air Force who had flown Flying Fortresses from there. Don was to be the Station Accountant Officer responsible for both Pay and Stores accounting staff and responsible directly to the Commanding Officer, who later when absent got him to take the morning station parade. It was on one of these parades that Don upset the Station Warrant Officer who accompanied him on inspection of the men. Walking along behind the centre rank he touched the back of an airman and said "haircut". The SWO immediately took out his book and asked the man's name, at which point Don intervened and told the SWO not to take the man's name. He soon realised what he had done and indeed regretted saying "haircut" as he had no wish to get someone on fatigues.

Soon after arriving at the station, someone at Command Headquarters warned him about the Commanding Officer, an ex air-gunner, telling him to be careful what he got involved in. Thus when he was asked by the CO whether it would be all right for the proceeds of letting blister hangers to farmers be shared by the messes, Don replied, "Yes, fine, providing Command gave their approval," which of course they had not.

Being an ex-American drome the accommodation on the station was good, in the excellent Officers' Mess a huge nude covered the wall behind the bar, whilst on the side walls was painted a record of all the raids the station had carried out and beside each one Swastikas showed how many enemy planes they claimed to have shot down. The RAF officers often made rude remarks about the latter but they were allowed to stay. Many of the officer huts had names over the doors and one name, familiar to everyone, was Major Clark Gable who flew on raids, or missions as the Americans would say, from this station. It seems he was there for some considerable time and had been a familiar figure at the local pub that more than once had to arrange transport to take him back to camp.

When not required to stay on camp as Orderly Officer, Don was able to go home at weekends, catching the run into Peterborough, twelve miles away, and then the fast train to Kings Cross. It was on one of these weekends that he had what he believed was his first encounter with telepathy. After one pay parade on a Friday, he had left his NCOs to balance the books for if he had stayed he would have missed the run into Peterborough. Next day his wife told him he had got out of bed during the night whilst still asleep and when she asked what he was doing he said he was looking for £4. 8s. 0d. She said she told him to get back to bed, which he did. When he got back to the station on Monday he was straightway told by the Sergeant in charge of Accounts that there had been a difference when balancing after the parade. When Don asked how much, he was told £4. 8s. 0d.

Of course he had no means of knowing this difference, or indeed that there was one, and certainly not how much it was. Thus on hearing the amount he immediately thought it must have come to him by telepathy at the time the difference was found. The staff of course that morning soon found where the error had occurred.

Another job he did whilst at Polebrook was to go with the CO to close a station at Sandy in Bedfordshire, and particularly to check stock and 'locking the gate'. They bought some of the wine and liquor stock for Polebrook before finally closing the station down.

After several months and near to his final release date, a big Mess dinner was arranged and he was able to invite Betty to come along. He arranged hotel accommodation for her in Peterborough and knew how worried she was as to what she could wear. However, everything went off well and the senior visiting officer, an Air Commodore and his wife, spent most of the evening with Don and Betty, so it all went down very well.

Don was at Polebrook right up to the time he had word that his demob replacement would be arriving and two days before he was due to leave a young officer arrived on station to learn what he had to do and take the reins over from him.

Chapter Twenty-Seven

Demob and back to 'civvy street'

He then had to report to Uxbridge for demob and soon after arrival was fitted out with a cheap suit and the obligatory hat, a trilby, which he would never wear. He had the standard demob leave plus an extra day for each month of service overseas; in all he had about three months due to him and in that time he was still considered to be in the service and thus could wear his uniform if he so wished. It was now the end of 1946 and his final leaving date was sometime in February, 1947.

Through no fault of his own he had not seen action but he was nevertheless proud of the service he had given. He had achieved officer status and left with the rank of flight lieutenant, equivalent to that of a captain in the Army. He now knew he would be returning to an office in a junior capacity whereas at Polebrook he had been responsible for a staff of twenty or thirty men and women doing work at least equivalent to that which he would now find himself doing on return to the Water Board. Before his leave ended he went back to work and at the request of women in the office went there one Saturday morning in his uniform. The uniform and a pilot's wings were very highly respected in wartime Britain and on one occasion when going along to the Spurs with Betty during a leave they were given two directors' box seats by a man seeing them queuing to go in.

The fact that he had been an officer of course made no difference in the office; he was still one of the juniors. Three men from the small pre-war staff had gone into the forces – one had become a lieutenant in the Navy and ended up commanding a minesweeper; another, old Smithy, had been killed as aircrew in the RAF and Don, who went as junior, returned as a junior. He was certainly brought down to earth when he was given the job of sticking notices on the windows of the offices reading 'WASTE NOT – WANT NOT'. His wartime contribution had been minimal but nevertheless it soon came home to him how people's attitude changed towards those who had been in the forces and how soon they forget. It reminded him of his childhood when he witnessed men standing in the kerb shaking uncontrollably or blind, selling matches or walking in the middle of the streets in the East End singing and hoping that the other poor of West Ham would give them a copper to get something to eat. He remembered his dad saying, "Yes, son, we all soon forget and don't want to know – it's human nature and, after all, everyone has his own troubles."

As yet Betty's sister's husband had not yet returned from the forces. Vera, his wife, lived next door and the poor girl had become very depressed and quite ill and had attempted suicide, Don and Betty helped her mother look after her. One day the doctor suggested she be taken to the Prince of Wales hospital in Tottenham, so Don took her along, but she refused the treatment they offered. A day or so later she became quite ill and violent and Don had to hold her down in bed until the doctor came and gave her a sedative. He then sent Don along to Tottenham town hall to get her certified as unwell so that she could have treatment in one of the mental hospitals for such people. She was taken to a hospital in Hertfordshire called Knapsbury. Shortly after getting her to hospital a telegram arrived to say her husband, Douglas, would be arriving at Waterloo station on his way back from the Middle East, where he had been with the 6th Airborne Division trying to keep the peace in Palestine. Don said he would meet him and give him the sad news, which he did and later went with him to Knapsbury hospital. Vera was there for almost six months and gradually got better, finally returning home and back to her old self.

Soon after leaving the forces Don got in touch with the Old Boys' Association to ask about football. Having been given the information he applied to the secretary who he had played with in the first eleven at school and found they were keen to get him to play for them. Thus most Saturdays in the winter months Don was playing, usually alternate weeks at the Enfield ground and then away to various teams throughout London. Most of the games were written up in the local paper and Don, playing at inside left, was frequently mentioned as he fairly regularly scored.

He was to carry on playing for them right through until he badly tore a cartilage in a cup game two or three years later. When the injury happened his team were winning 4-0 but after he went off, the ten men (there were no substitutes in those days) could not hold the other side and the match ended in a draw. Don went to hospital with his injury, a badly torn cartilage, but was told they would not operate, which they would have done if he had been a professional, and that he would have to wait for it to heal. His team went on to win the Old Boys' Cup. The team secretary sent him a ticket for the England versus Scotland game at Wembley and he went along to see England lose 3-1 with the usual crowd of 100,000 present for this game. His cartilage injury turned out to be the end of his playing career and then for many years he became a regular spectator at White Hart Lane watching Tottenham Hotspurs' every home game for some years. He had earlier, in fact in 1948, queued with his sister to get tickets for the FA Cup semi final held at Villa Park and went with his dad by train to Birmingham, only to see his side lose to Blackpool who fielded, among others, Stanley Matthews.

Although the war had ended the forces were still engaged in fighting overseas, this time in Malaya where Chinese communists inhabiting the country tried to turn the whole of the Malayan peninsular communist. The fighting was to continue for many years before victory was finally gained by the British.

Football played a big part in Don's life and although there were far fewer internationals for England in those days not always played at Wembley, he managed to get to some of the important ones at that venue, of course as a standing spectator. One international played at White Hart Lane he particularly remembered. It was against Italy when for the first time an English crowd were treated to some fancy ball play before the game, tricks with the ball that today are common place and are only able to be done because of the boots now worn and presumably then by the Italians. The crowd, Don amongst them, after seeing this display, must have thought that England would be on a hiding to nothing. Not the case, England won easily without all this new fancy ball play.

Betty had for some time been working in the City, her office having moved back from their country mansion soon after the war ended. She travelled up to town by trolleybus whilst Don, having 'lost' his bicycle whilst away in the forces, also went by public transport to his office in nearby Tottenham. Don and his wife occupied two top rooms in Betty's mother's house and set about decorating and buying furniture. The standard furniture in post-war Britain was known as 'utility' furniture, all built in a plain wood finish without any veneer. However, when out one day shopping in Tottenham they spotted a number of people looking in a shop window and going over to see what it was all about they saw two men just putting the finishing touches to a bedroom display which featured a suite of polished wood on what was clearly utility furniture, so unlike the furniture usually in the shops at this time. He and Betty quickly went into the shop and asked about the bedroom suite just put into the window. They were told it was the first of a new batch of veneered furniture made locally which they were now permitted to sell. Without asking the price, Don already knew the price of utility furniture was controlled, he said they would have it, the shopkeeper telling them they would have to pay extra for the walnut veneer finish. The price of a utility bedroom suite was £47 and consisted of a 4 foot 6 inches bed, a headboard, tallboy, dressing table and large wardrobe. The addition for veneer, £20, was much more than Don had anticipated, but they so wanted it that he did not quibble.

About this time Don's sister married again, this time to a painter/decorator who had lived all his life in the East End. Everyone, including Don, liked Eric and after living at his parents' house for a time they managed to get a house in the new town at Harlow.

Over the next two or three years whilst Don still worked at the Tottenham office his life continued without any major happenings. Work at the office continued as before and Don entered his ledger, sent out his notices and when payment was not received went as usual out 'on the district' to collect or when fed up with calling and listening to 'why should I pay water rates?', threatening to cut off supply and, when this did not work, then calling the bad guy's bluff and getting Water Board men to dig up the pavement and cut off. No one who could genuinely not afford to pay would be so treated but some people are determined to be awkward and nasty and eventually after months are cut off, when they always immediately paid the rate plus the extra cost incurred in the cutting off.

A very amusing incident occurred one evening on his way home from work that he and his friends with him would always remember. Catching a trolley bus at a stop near the office, Don and two friends went upstairs as usual, the bus did not have many passengers up there this time of day. Don sat by himself on a seat in front of the two friends and was turning round talking to them when there was an almighty explosion accompanied by the shattering of glass. Opposite to where they were sitting there had appeared a great hole in the glass and the immediate thought was that someone had thrown a brick through the window. The bus had pulled up with a jerk and a little man sitting next to the broken window turned to Don and friends and said, "Take no notice." The conductor came running up the stairs and walking down the aisle said, "Who did that? Now come on who did it?" The little man sank further into the collar of his overcoat and said nothing. The conductor was looking at everyone suspiciously and Don and his friends had difficulty in restraining themselves from laughing. Finally the little man, with the conductor towering over him, spoke, "I did it!" The conductor looked at him in amazement, "Cor blimey, how did you do that?"

"Well you see, there was that wasp and I hit him with me cap."

"Christ, some mothers do have 'em," he paused and then in a loud authoritative voice, "Right now, everybody off the bus, this bus is now out of commission."

As Don and friends got up to leave the little man got out his Identity Card offering it to the conductor. "I expect you want this," he said in such a way as if he knew the procedure because he had done it before.

For some time after, the three had many laughs in the office when hearing an unusual noise, one of them was sure to say, "Take no notice!"

Don and Betty went on a two-week holiday each year, mostly to the Isle of Wight, by train from Waterloo, but once to Swanage in Dorset. The journey to the 'Island' from Waterloo on a Saturday morning was always quite an event and was started by joining the long queue stretching outside the station and down Waterloo Road. But one did not have too long to wait as the trains ran one after the other, packed tight so that when you got to Portsmouth you were bundled out onto the platform and waited where you were, as there was no room to move either way, until the ferry that always seemed to be present unloaded its bronzed passengers and the new pale-faced arrivals were allowed to board.

Evenings at home were spent listening to the wireless, sometimes with Don trying to study, or else going to the pictures or to a dance, in the latter case usually with Betty's sister Vera and her husband or with her cousin Jean and her boyfriend Frank. Once a week they visited Don's parents. At weekends they often visited or had a visit from Don's best man, Ron, and his family, after perhaps going for a walk locally.

One day Betty's mother said the landlord of the house had approached her through his agent to see if she would like to buy the property. The government had put controls on rents and the landlord was only getting the same rent he had been receiving for many years. Don's mother-in-law was a widow and could not entertain the idea of buying and wondered if Don would like to buy. It seems that George, her second son who had been badly wounded in Italy, and who lived in the house did not want to buy. Don could see this was a good opportunity as he knew the asking price would not be great, as the rent the landlord was receiving was only twelve shillings a week. The house was an end of terrace Victorian house built in 1881 and on three floors. Don had a talk to the agent and they agreed on a price of £425. Don had previously been in touch with the council and found the house was on a list for development but was assured it would not be for about twenty years. (As a matter of interest certainly in 2006, nearly sixty years later, the house was still there, unfortunately not now owned by Don.) Thus he acquired his first house for comparatively little money and at the same time was able to claim war damage from the government which was eventually carried out to the value of £500! The damage was due to the bomb which had fallen in 1941 and the house he had bought had had some superficial damage. He had bought a nine-room house for £425 and had the government pay for war damage worth £500.

Chapter Twenty-Eight

It was in 1948 that he went out one Saturday morning with the intention of buying a radiogram but instead came back having bought a television set at the London Co-op. It was the first set he had seen in England since first seeing one with his parents above a shop in Enfield just before the war. It was one of the first sets to be sold in Tottenham, post war, and as far as he knew there were none for sale in Edmonton. It cost £90, a very large sum of money in today's terms, and had a nine-inch tube and twenty-one valves, and after a few days it kept breaking down, the tube and valves being changed several times at no cost to him. Programmes on television started about eight o'clock each night and Don and Betty became so absorbed in watching each evening that they almost stopped going to the pictures and dances as they had usually done. Also, since no one they knew had a set there were often people coming round to see it, particularly at weekends when first division football and cup matches were shown.

Early in '48 the Spurs got to the semi final of the FA Cup and were to play Blackpool at Villa Park. As was mentioned above, Don and his sister queued at White Hart Lane for hours to get two tickets as he wanted to take his father. There were over twenty thousand going up to Birmingham from north London and there were hundreds of coaches but of course Don and his dad went by one of the many excursion trains from Euston. When they arrived, hours before the game, there was much fun walking around the town and meeting supporters of the opposing team, it was all very friendly. Many people on both sides had dressed up in fancy clothes for the occasion and when two opposing parties met in the street there was much friendly banter passing between the two lots of people. It was an exciting game with over 70,000 in the crowd but unfortunately Blackpool won, largely due to the top-class footballer Stanley Matthews.

For the cup final that year Don and Betty had nine people watching their small television screen, some of the friends coming a good distance from their homes. The big event that followed in the same year was the Olympic Games held at Wembley, covered by BBC television, and Don took off a couple of days from work in order to see some of the events on his television. He also bought two tickets for Wembley and took his dad along to one day's events, the big one that day was the 1500 metres. Most of Wembley Stadium was without seating for football matches but since people were generally going to be there for several hours during an Olympic day the number of tickets were limited to allow people to sit on the terraces, the only cover at Wembley being at the sides where there was proper seating. It had rained on the day they went and people had to sit on damp concrete and going home it was easy to spot those on the underground who had been to see the games as they all had wet seats.

Sometime towards the end of the forties Don was moved back up to Head Office, first working in the General Section where wages and pensions were paid. It was whilst there he found a quick way to find tax payable by individuals and got it introduced into the section. It was also in this section whilst with several others seated round a long table opening the morning post he made a prediction, amazing those present the next day as it came true. There was always general chatter around the table and on this occasion the talk was of the big fight to take place that night. Boxing was more important in the sporting world in those days and the big fight between a highly ranked American and the British Heavyweight Champion was headline news. The American was expected to win but Don said he knew the American would be knocked out in the fourth round. Everyone laughed and he was asked how he had come to this conclusion and there was even more laughter when he said he had dreamed it.

That evening he was in his bed studying and half listening to the boxing commentary on the wireless when suddenly a roar went up and it was obvious the fight had ended and as predicted the British boxer had knocked out his opponent in the fourth round. Next morning at work everyone was telling him he ought to do the pools and asking in fun who was going to win the three o'clock at Sandown. It was going to be some years later that Don read in the paper the same American boxer, now on hard times and obviously in need of money, gave a story to an American paper that he took a dive when he had fought the British Heavyweight Champion. It was obvious the story was not believed as it only merited a few lines in the middle of the paper. However, Don believed it as he felt sure he must have somehow tuned into the fixing of the fight whilst he was asleep – this his second telepathic experience.

In 1950 one of the young lads in his department who had been called up for National Service came into the office to tell his friends he was off out East, no doubt to Korea where a war had started with American and British forces involved. It all seemed so unreal and strangely very much more remote to those at home than anything in the last war, who had only a few years before begun to enjoy peace and begin to get back to normality, even still with some rationing. The difference was that this war was unlikely to affect so many people and unlike the last war there was no threat of casualties amongst civilians. It of course was very real to the young lad and his family and Don did not remember whether he returned unharmed.

Whilst in General Section he formed a football team, Fryer's Floosies (Fryer being the section boss), and they played two or three games against other departments and won all. One summer they played cricket and apart from being a wicket taker Don managed by some fluke to be top scorer with 12 runs!

After a year or two, in fact in the summer of 1951, he was transferred to another section, this time Expenditure Examination. All through the post-war years at Tottenham and later in General Section, Don had been studying for the examinations of the Chartered Institute of Secretaries, taking one exam after another, until he finally passed out as an associate member. After a brief spell in the new department he was chosen to work on the audit of a large contract the Water Board had with John Mowlem, builder, for the construction of a filtration works at Sunbury on Thames. His job was to work with the contractors, making sure they charged fairly since the contract was a variation of cost plus. It took him just over two hours to get to the building site by public transport but luckily was expected to go there only two or three times a week. He worked well with Mowlem's staff and enjoyed being there, often in the open air, and learnt a lot about building work both from the architects and the engineers. The plant he was told would be the biggest of its kind in Europe and had already been under construction for three years. However, there was a shortage of building workers and although huts for men to live in had been built to accommodate 600 there were never more than 300 men on site.

He wanted, however, to leave the Water Board, preferably to go into industry, as his time in the services had made him more ambitious but although he had succeeded in becoming an associate of the Chartered Institute of Secretaries he found that this was not sufficient to get any company interested in employing him after working so long for a public undertaking, often frowned upon by people working in industry. So, since he wanted to get further in life and knew that although his job was nice and safe, in the Water Board it was a case of dead man's shoes with promotion and rewards being very slow in coming, he had decided to try for an additional qualification, this time it was to be the Cost and Works Accountants. So, as long as he could keep awake, he spent most of his time when travelling to and from his new job, studying the papers he had received from the new correspondence course he had paid for from a company who called themselves Rapid Results. There would be four examinations and even with partial exemption from part, due to his present qualification, there would still be new subjects to study and the correspondence course thought he should allow three years to complete. Don, however, was determined to get everything out of the way in eighteen months. He thus had to work hard.

Chapter Twenty-Nine

In 1952, whilst working at Ashford Common, the name of the new filtration plant, he and Betty thought they ought to get a car and thus when the motor show arrived at Earls Court they went along to see what might be on offer. Very few young people had a car at that time but judging by the number of people at the show many more would soon have. The biggest crowd was around the Ford stand who it seems were introducing a new car, the Consul. This was in Don's price range, providing he could pay over a couple of years, and so he pushed his way through to ask one of the Ford men what one did to get one.

"You go along to a dealer who sells Fords and put your name down on a waiting list."

"How long is one expected to wait?" Don asked.

"If you join the list now it will be about five years."

Thus a new car for Betty and Don was out of the question so Don started looking at adverts for used cars and eventually went along to a garage in Tottenham to see what they had. He had almost decided on one second-hand car but when walking back to the office with the salesman he spotted the new car in the window, a Morris Minor. Don had chatted about the war when talking to the salesman who had also been in the RAF.

"That's what I would really like," Don said pointing to the Morris, knowing, however, it was out of the question as he had heard their waiting list for this new model was just as long as the Ford.

"Come inside. I might be able to help you."

Don was surprised but tried not to show it.

"Providing you keep your mouth shut I may be able to let you have it. I'm getting fed up with writing to people on my list and finding they have gone away or have already bought another car. When I sell this one, Morris will let me have another one. So if you keep it to yourself you can have it."

Don was amazed, paid the deposit, signed a hire purchase agreement and was told the car would be delivered as soon as it had been serviced.

While at Ashford Common one of his Mowlem friends whose father was a bookmaker, also arranging fights at the Manor Place Baths in London, told many there that his father had found a very good heavyweight boxer. It seemed the man was a milkman and in the few bouts arranged for him had quickly knocked out all his opponents. The man, Dick Richardson, the Mowlem man said, was going to be the next British Heavyweight Champion. Later he told Don that the next fight would be on the wireless and sure enough Don and his dad listened and to their surprise the new boxer won by a quick knockout, he was definitely on his way. This was at the time of Henry Cooper and Joe Erskine and although Richardson did not become British Heavyweight Champion he became the champion of Europe but never made the World title, but it was interesting following the man's progress knowing one was privy to him early in his career.

Although a pilot Don had never driven a car and thus, a few weeks before getting the Morris, he had taken a couple of lessons, when after some short instruction the instructor mostly sat talking to him about the war as he said there is no way he would fail the test. So he applied for the test, took it and failed after rolling back on a hill start. He told Betty what had happened and said he knew he would be failed directly it happened – "The driving test man was quite right in failing me, I must make sure I don't do that again." So when the Morris arrived he could only drive it accompanied by a driver with a licence. Anyway he got Frank, Betty's cousin's boyfriend, to accompany him and straightway applied again for another test.

The day for the test arrived and Frank said he would go along with him, providing Don took him to Twickenham

157

afterwards to see the Rugby international against France. Frank played in one of the Saracens' teams. Thus the test completed and passed, he took Frank to see the match, the only rugby international Don had seen.

Soon after he had been moved to head office an ex-Army major in General Section had got him to join the Water Board section of the British Legion and although not attending any meetings he nevertheless joined the small group who on Armistice Day paraded in front of the memorial in the building. Unfortunately the first year's parade became a shambles as, on the major's order to dismiss, some had forgotten which way to turn and one or two ended up facing each other – it made a good laugh.

Over the next year and a half the car was used a lot, Don taking people for rides since hardly anyone he knew had a car. In 1953 they toured the Highlands of Scotland, sleeping in the car to save money. He also showed his new car to his friends at Ashford Common and found he could get there in just over half the time it took him by public transport. However, he needed to study, which he did on the train, and the public transport fare was partly recoverable from the Water Board so he only rarely used the car.

One of the special events in that year was when he went by car to another Spurs FA Cup semi final, again at Villa Park, and once again against Blackpool, who had beaten them in 1948. Don and his sister again queued for hours, starting at five in the morning, to get tickets and whilst they were in the queue Don's friend Del came along and they managed to get the kind people around to let him join them in the queue; probably it helped telling them Del had carried out over 60 raids over Germany in the war. The ticket his sister queued for was for their father and, having offered Del a ride up to Birmingham, it was the three men who went up there to watch Matthews, five years later, again destroy the hopes of Tottenham getting in the final.

It was probably the journey up to Birmingham and a later one with friends down to Devon that prompted Don to consider looking for a larger more comfortable car. In view of the good deal Don had got when buying the car he knew that the second-hand price would be good and having found out that a new Austin A40 could now be bought for little more than the money he would get for the Morris, they decided to make a change. They had planned to go again to the Highlands for a holiday and would go off in the Austin when it arrived. But it did not arrive as promised and Don had already handed the Morris over to the garage. The garage, however, agreed to lend him a car. It was a Standard Vanguard, a far superior car than either the Morris or the Austin. They therefore toured Scotland in a much superior car and both agreed it would be nice to have one like this. Don asked at the garage and was told that for a little extra they could get him a new Vanguard and forget the Austin. So this is what happened.

The Korean War had ended just after Don had bought his Morris Minor and still the tension between East and West continued.

Betty's sister, Vera, and her husband, now with two small boys, had moved to a house on an estate at Cheshunt in Hertfordshire and one evening the devastating news came that Vera had been found dead by her niece, having taken her own life. They straightway went over to see what could be done, Don helping Douglas lay out his wife. It was a very traumatic time for all and it took some time before things got back to normal.

Chapter Thirty

The following year Don as planned completed the exams for his new qualification and became an associate member of the Institute of Cost and Works Accountants, which he felt sure would now give him a better chance of a move from The Metropolitan Water Board. Later that year their son was born but within a few days Betty became depressed and wanted nothing to do with the baby. A doctor was called and he decided that she must have treatment in much the same way as her sister had had a few years before. Betty was taken by Don and an aunt to Hill End hospital near St Albans.

Fortunately for him he was living in the same house as his mother-in-law and she took over caring for the baby whilst he was at work. On his return from work and after a meal prepared by Betty's mother, he each evening took over caring for the baby putting him in the cot next to his bed.

He visited Betty in hospital some evenings and at weekends. Betty was given ECT (Electro Convulsive Therapy) and a lot of insulin and gradually got better. However, it was almost six months before they thought she was well enough to come home to stay, although near the end of her time there she had been allowed home for a weekend. Her doctor at the hospital recommended that they seriously consider moving from the district as he felt a complete change would help recovery.

It was about this time that several Hungarians came to live in Britain following their failed uprising against Russia in 1956. The tension with the Soviet Union thus continued.

So now that Betty was well again, Don again wrote for work in industry and very soon was invited for an interview with a company in Rugby. The interview was a success and he was offered the job as an assistant internal auditor in the British

Thompson Houston Company, a company which employed thousands in Rugby and elsewhere in the UK. Going to work in Rugby meant he would have to be in digs until he could find a house for his family. Betty came with him one weekend to look around and they put a deposit on a small detached house being built on a large estate.

People at the Water Board were most surprised that Don was going to leave after almost eighteen years, since he had first joined them before the war. He of course had to give a month's notice and when finally the day arrived for him to leave they made him a presentation attended by many of the people he had known for years. The man who had interviewed him all those years ago made the presentation saying how brave everyone thought he was to leave after such a long time. Don made a speech and said he would certainly miss many things, such as the annual athletic meeting where only recently he had run in the three-mile handicap race and where, because of his football skills, they had handicapped him almost a lap behind some at the front. Then there were the meetings with many friends in the pub after football or cricket matches. Yes, he would miss a lot but he had already got over missing the many laughs and friendship of the Tottenham Office, so he knew he would soon forget the present tugs as he gave his final speech.

The BTH in Rugby found digs for him and going along to inspect he found that there were about ten apprentices living in the house being looked after for breakfast and evening meal by the lady of the house; he had to share a room with one of the young men. He discovered that in addition to the apprentices living in Rugby town there were another 500 living in a hostel close by, which was full. The hours of work at the office were quite different from those he had been used to at the Water Board, starting now at eight thirty and staying until six, all office staff were treated the same as the thousands of factory workers and all had to clock in and out.

He was able to get home at weekends travelling on the LMS mainline to Euston, all trains he caught were fast to London. On returning early on Monday morning the most convenient train he found was on the LNER service from Marylebone to their station in Rugby. The line from Marylebone passed through many towns new to him, the train arriving in time for him to walk down to the factory and clock in. The Factory Auditor had employed four qualified accountants as he said he would be taking over very soon as Company Secretary from the then present ageing Secretary. The company had not hitherto employed qualified accountants and Don's boss wanted this well-established company, from a manufacturing point of view, to get up to date in Administration and Accounting. Don found he and the others had little to do as they were additional to the audit staff already employed and who had been retained. They were in effect waiting for the big change to be made. In the first few weeks he visited one or two factories with a senior member of the department but apart from this much of his time was spent talking with others in he department who had little to do, all awaiting the forthcoming promotion of their immediate boss. Don did, however, enjoy one of his visits to a factory in Nelson and Colne, Lancashire, as the senior member he went with took him along to Burnley Football ground (Turf Moor) where he had lunch and met several people.

The new estate on which his house was being built had previously been farm land close to the main railway line from Euston. Several roads had been completed and the three-bedroom detached house they had put their money on would soon be finished. The mortgage had been arranged through a local agent and the cost of the house was £2,000.

Back at the digs he became friendly with a couple of the young lads and spent one or two evenings out with them but mostly he stayed in the lounge with others playing cards or just talking. The lads there were all much younger than him. Most of the apprentices at some time had to attend evening school and Don learnt from a young man in his office, who was studying Company Law, that the teacher had left and there was now no one to take over. Don had himself studied Company Law and having, when down in London, seriously thought of teaching at evening school, perhaps economics, said he would offer his services to the school. Thus it was arranged for him to meet the headmaster who accepted him for the job. The school was The Rugby College of Technology and Art. Initially of course he had to get out his books and study before taking his first class and such became the pattern on some nights each week so that he was hopefully prepared for the questions put to him by eager young apprentices. He found he enjoyed the two evenings a week at school.

One day at work much to his surprise he found he had a chance to once again play a game of football when he learnt the offices were to play the factory. Don put his name forward, and was accepted after a short trial. The game played on the factory pitch was keenly fought and his side managed to win, but unlike so many games when playing several years earlier, he did not score.

It was about three months after starting in Rugby that the bombshell was dropped – his boss, on whose promotion Don's future prospects in the company depended, did not get the position of Company Secretary he had said he was certain to get. In fact the present secretary had retired as expected but instead of appointing one person to take over his work as previously carried out, the board had decided to divide the work between two men who had been employed in the company for many years. His boss would therefore no longer be destined for senior management and the four qualified accountants he had employed would no longer be in line for the jobs they had been promised. It was time to move on, Don was devastated; he had given up a secure job and pension in the Water Board where he had been employed, including war service, for nearly eighteen years, and was now having to seek work elsewhere. At the time there was no question of him getting notice to leave, it was just that prospects in the company were now much reduced. Don, at thirty-four years of age, was much older than the three other men employed with him and they certainly had not given up such secure employment to work there. All four started looking at job vacancies, three for work in the Midlands whilst Don concentrated on jobs further south.

He had a favourable reply from a company in Surrey where he had applied for the position of an assistant accountant; they wanted him for an interview. He received the letter just at the time he was going home to help Betty with the move up to Rugby as the house they had bought was now ready for occupation; he had taken a day's leave for the move. He arrived home to find the removal van already loading and broke the news to Betty that he had to arrange an interview with a company in Surrey. They decided they would have to go ahead with moving up to Rugby but agreed he should take the interview. So off he went to the telephone call box across the road to talk to the Surrey company.

The move up to Rugby went smoothly and Don arranged an interview at the new company for the following week. Betty seemed to enjoy being in her new home and certainly liked Rugby, as indeed Don did too, but they both knew they were almost certainly going to have to move again. The interview with the company in Surrey, held in a big country mansion which the company had taken over at the beginning of the war, went well and afterwards Don was taken along to the Company Secretary's house in a smart private road nearby. He was then driven to Woking to see one of the factories owned by the company and to meet the Managing Director as this, if he got the job, he was told is where he would eventually be working. He must have impressed the MD he met there because it was hinted that the job might well be his. On the way back to Weybridge the Company Secretary suggested he might like to bring along his wife for coffee the following Saturday to see if she approved of where he would be working. This seemed strange to him but whether they wanted to check on his family or whether they were simply being friendly, he was not sure. He had no second thoughts about bringing Betty along as he knew she was well liked by whoever she met. So on the following Saturday they left Rugby early, drove down to London and left the baby with Betty's mother before driving to Weybridge in Surrey. There they were entertained to coffee and the meeting was obviously a great success as it was arranged that Don would start work in Weybridge one month later after giving the required notice to leave the factory in Rugby.

Chapter Thirty-One

Another new beginning

Now he would have to sell the house in Rugby and look for somewhere to live in Surrey. The new company agreed they would arrange accommodation for him until he found suitable accommodation locally. He was to be looked after in another country mansion owned by the company, next to the one in which he had been interviewed. Thus once again he would have to be in digs. The house in Rugby was put on the market and he arranged for Betty to have her mother stay with her up there for a time. Betty said she was quite happy living in Rugby and would be sorry to leave.

Betty had a friend who lived in Woking not far from the offices where Don would shortly be working and she wrote to her to see if she knew of any new developments in the area where they might find a house. Having moved into a new house in Rugby both Betty and Don were keen to find another new house rather than a second-hand one. The friend, Thelma, who used to live in Edmonton and a year or so earlier had been travelling daily with Betty to the City where they both worked, came back with two developments in the Woking area. So, on the first Saturday they drove down to Woking to look at the places Thelma had told them about. It did not take them long to decide on one development and to agree to buy a small three-bedroom detached house there, the Company Secretary of the new company having previously agreed to arrange the mortgage they would require. The house was not yet completed and it would be a few weeks before they could take possession.

The month of notice in Rugby soon went by and Don went down south to work in Surrey. The bedroom he was given in the country mansion was excellent and he was to be looked after for evening meal and breakfast by the lady in charge of providing dinners during the day for all staff who worked in this and the main house next door; she had an apartment in the house.

Don was to be the assistant to the accountant for the group which he discovered consisted of a holding company and a number of subsidiaries. The main house itself had been converted into offices and in addition several huts had been erected in the vast grounds to accommodate many other workers, including draughtsmen, engineers, chemists, accounts and other office employees.

The Group Accountant, Arthur K, reporting directly to the Company Secretary, Roberts, was a Chartered Accountant. Don found it strange doing basic accounting work for the first time, for although he had been an accountant officer in the RAF, entered simple rate ledgers in the Water Board, and assisted in auditing internal work in a large factory, all his knowledge of basic accounting work, purchase ledgers, sales ledgers, profit and loss accounts etc. had been acquired from books studied for his qualifications. He wished he had had at least some short experience in such work when he would have acquired the special methods and tricks used by experienced staff. However, Don bluffed his way through and no one seemed to know.

Each weekend he drove back up to Rugby, returning on the Monday after leaving early enough to get to the office by nine. He found the quickest and shortest route down did not touch any large towns and passed through much lovely English countryside and villages, it was especially enjoyable and free from traffic when riding down early on a Monday morning. There were no motorways in those days.

The weeks passed and Don soon found he had made many friends and often at lunch times took walks with some in the pleasant country lanes close to the offices, whilst chatting and putting the world to right. He particularly liked his room in the big house where waking up in the morning it seemed as if he were in a foreign country with the sounds of the countryside all around. One day in the office he was asked to order some stationery and was told a man would shortly be along to see him. When the man arrived Don was shocked to see it was Alec Bedser, the England cricketer, who he soon learnt had opened a shop with his brother, Eric, selling office equipment. He never asked him for his autograph, treating him almost as if he did not know who he was as he felt this was the way the man would best appreciate it. He did kick himself afterwards as he knew his son would have liked to have had the autograph when he grew up.

In April the house in Woking was finished and ready for occupation. The house in Rugby had been on the market for several weeks but had not sold, so Don moving down to Surrey would have to be paying two mortgages. The move down went without a hitch and Betty was soon making friends with neighbours in the road. Finally the house in Rugby was sold much to Don's relief as the mortgage on the Woking house was already more than the one in Rugby and yet the money he earned was about the same. The house had been bought for the sum of £3,200 whilst the one in Rugby sold for £2,000. Don was on a salary of £900 a year.

As an added bonus to his move he was pleased to find that the local football team, Woking, were doing quite well in one of the top amateur leagues, and he started going along to see them on a Saturday.

After some nine months working in Weybridge he was moved to the factory in Woking he had visited when first interviewed. At the new factory he was now Accountant for that company, a major subsidiary in a group of some fourteen companies, with the task of building a small accounts department for that company. He started interviewing for staff almost immediately having previously seen, whilst working in the Weybridge office, that advertisements were placed for staff needed. Four of the staff appointed came from within the company having already been dealing with and recording bought and sales invoices. Don soon found out that he had made a good choice in the appointment of Chief Clerk as the young lady had been there only a short time when she had on her own initiative organised the department to his satisfaction.

He soon got into the routine of working in the new surroundings and found everyone helpful and friendly. The company manufactured metal plating equipment and had a chemical department which made and sold the chemicals used in plating. The main customers were of course the motor industry which included the many small companies in the Birmingham and Coventry areas who plated small parts for the motor giants. Don spent part of the first few weeks familiarising himself with the factory and the various departments in the company including the drawing office and engineers' offices. He knew he would have to work closely with all departments if he wanted to get them to give him all he needed to be able to give the Managing Director a monthly account of how the business was doing. He met all the heads of departments and all were soon on first name terms. At the end of the second month he was able to produce a set of internal accounts, the first the MD had ever had, and a break-even chart which the MD found most helpful. He had settled in well and got on well with everyone.

At home Betty's recovery from her illness had continued well and young Stephen was crawling around and being taken for long walks to the shops in the pushchair. Weekend shopping with dad was either to Woking or sometimes to Guildford but as Betty did not drive her mid-week ventures to the shops was to the nearest village, West Byfleet.

As far as football was concerned, in 1958 Woking made their way to the final of the Amateur Cup; in those days held at Wembley before big crowds. Don having seen most of their cup games bought a ticket for the final and, as not many in the road had cars, offered to take two men he knew in his car. Woking, playing Ilford, won 2-1 before a crowd of 71,000.

An amendment to the Rent Restriction Act had recently caused his parents to move home from the house he had left to go into the RAF, and where he had been when the V2 rocket had landed opposite. They had moved to the new town of Harlow where his sister and her husband had a year or two before taken a house. The journey over to Harlow from Woking was tedious; the distance was just over fifty miles but having to travel across London even though using the North Circular Road, took nearly two and a half hours each way. Don, Betty and the little boy made the journey as often as they could find the time.

Betty managed to persuade her mother and grandmother who lived with her to come over to stay for a while. Betty had told her grandmother, a lady who had lived all her life in north London, about the squirrels that ran amongst the trees at the end of the garden and the old lady in her nineties spent much of each day looking out of the window but for some reason the squirrels never appeared. The next guests at the house were Don's parents who stayed with them for a few days, Don's father had recently retired having been working for the railway for 48 years, retiring on a pension, for which he had paid in sixpence a week, of only 14 shillings a week!

At work he was making good progress and had fitted in well with the company, the MD often talking to him and thanking him for what he was doing. However, he had left the Water Board to try to better himself and here he was earning no more than he had done some three years before. He was now confident in what he was capable of doing and resolved to look elsewhere for employment. He saw an advertisement for a position with a company in Ascot which was within a reasonable distance from his present home. The job was for Chief Accountant at a small company and from the way the advertisement read the salary and prospects would be good. Don applied and a week later he was called for interview. The new company was very obliging and obviously interested and agreed to a Saturday interview.

Don met the Managing Director and was taken around the factory and offices and got along well with the few people who were in working on that Saturday. He was offered the job and the boss of the company said he would write to him setting down salary etc.

Two days later the letter arrived, the salary was to be just over twice that he was earning and there would be a directorship. The company, although small, was quoted on the London Stock Exchange. After talking it over with Betty it was decided he would give in his notice the following day and that initially at least he would commute to Ascot. He duly wrote out his notice and handed it to the director who looked after staff matters. The man was obviously annoyed and asked why he had not told them he was not satisfied and seeking new employment, but Don told him in no uncertain manner that he did not expect to have to ask for more money that it was up to them to pay him what they felt he was worth. He went back to his office and within an hour was called to see the MD and the staff director. It became clear they did not want to lose him and the MD said he had spoken to the Group MD and that they would increase his salary immediately to a figure close to that Don had told them he was being offered by the new company. He thanked them and said he would discuss it with his wife and let them know the next day.

That evening he and Betty talked until late at night trying to decide what to do. He had verbally accepted the Ascot job and felt awkward about letting the man down who had made him such a generous offer; however, in the end they decided it would be marginally better to accept the revised salary in his present company on the basis of 'the devil you know'. The following morning he rang the company in Ascot and told them what had happened; the MD there was most understanding and wished him the best of luck. He then told his present employers that he had decided to accept their new offer.

He was now, at least in his mind, well off; his salary meant he would now be receiving net nearly twice that which he had been getting, and would now have money to buy that cine camera he had been looking at in Woking.

Chapter Thirty-Two

Shortly after his good luck he had the sad news that his father had had a heart attack. He and Betty went over with Stephen, now almost four years old, to see 'granddad' in hospital in Bishop Stortford. His dad appeared to be getting better but a few days later the message came that his mother had been asked by the police to go to the hospital. Don drove over to Harlow right away and took his mother to the hospital but his father had died, in fact although the police had not said so he must have already been dead when they passed on the message to go to the hospital. After the funeral, held in Enfield, he brought his mother back to Woking to stay for a while.

The company continued to make good profits and grow, so Don's department was forced to get bigger. He employed extra staff and engaged an assistant accountant who although unqualified had had considerable experience working for a firm of accountants. The man picked turned out to be a good choice and Don even persuaded him to start studying again.

It was soon obvious that the company thought they had made the right decision in increasing his salary as he became more and more involved in matters outside the work of his department and people were always coming to him for advice. The company had apparently interested Mitsubishi through the company's agent in France, in the 'know how' for a piece of equipment for galvanising massive rolls of metal, called a stripline; the agent had been the man they used when selling the same 'know how' to France. There was, it seemed, a contractual problem with the Japanese and the MD asked Don if he would go to their London office to sort it out

He felt most uncomfortable going to talk to Japanese, after all not many years before his country had been at war with them and while in the forces he had been shown Japanese atrocity films and since the war he had resolved not to buy anything from that country. However, he said nothing of this and went. He met the Japanese and reworded a contract document to their satisfaction. Some months later the French agent asked the MD to meet him and some Japanese at lunch somewhere in town and to bring along a sum of money that no doubt the agent had promised someone to seal the contract. The MD asked Don to accompany him and to make arrangements with their bank to collect $10,000 to be handed over to the company's agent.

They duly met at the restaurant, Don armed with the money, only to be told before sitting down to the meal that the money was wanted in one-dollar bills. So Don had to ring the bank and then go across to their bank to collect a small case of notes. He arrived back in time to at least enjoy some of the meal and indeed was invited by one of the Japanese present to visit them in Japan.

Chapter Thirty-Three

During the next few years Don made several visits to the company's Manchester and Birmingham offices and also visits to factories of important customers, sometimes just as a courtesy visit but often to sign contracts. He particularly enjoyed his visits to Prestige in Lancashire and to Raleigh in Nottingham where he was given a complete tour of the factory.

So the years rolled on and there came a time when the MD decided to send him to London to be assessed by outside consultants. The main person to interview him was a qualified accountant with an engineering degree. The session lasted all day with Don answering all the questions put forward which he was told were tests devised by a Dutch professor. He apparently performed well, particularly when he was given the task of moving trucks, or freight cars, in a railway marshalling yard. They told him he had done the task faster than anyone had previously carried it out; Don laughingly told them he had had an advantage as his father had been an engine driver on the railway and shunting trains was second nature.

It was not long after this that he was appointed Company Secretary for his company, a post previously held at Group Headquarters, and of course there were further salary increases.

At home his son, Stephen, was getting near the age for school, the nearest being some mile and a half away, something they had not thought about when choosing the house when moving down from Rugby. However, Betty discovered that a special bus stopped near the end of the road to pick up children for a small private school in Woking. So now that Don was doing well at work they decided to see if they could get a place for Stephen at the private school. They went along for an interview and a place was arranged. The fee was £30 a term, which they could well afford.

The family continued to make visits to both Harlow and Edmonton and from time to time they entertained both their mothers, now both widows. One day Don came home from work to find that the gentleman he had stayed with in Canada, Mr Hutson, and with whom he had kept up correspondence, was there with his new wife; his previous wife who had looked after Don and his friends so well at Christmas 1943 had unfortunately died a few years before. The Hutsons stayed over for a few days.

On another day when returning home from work Don was in for a big surprise. His mother was staying with them and Betty had arranged a small coffee morning and his mother in chatting to one of the neighbours at the house had discovered that two doors away the lady's husband had gone to the same school as Don in Essex.

"Did you know anyone with the name Pip Foster when at school?" his mother asked.

"Yes, I knew him well, he was in the same class and I played football with him for the school. Why do you ask?"

"He lives next door but one to you and has been living there for two years."

Don duly met the neighbour a few days later but they had never been particularly friendly as Pip was one of the 'posh' boys from the Gidea Park area whilst Don had been one of the 'rough' boys from Dagenham. Betty did, however, become very friendly with Pip's wife, a very likeable lady, unlike her husband who always seemed a little aloof.

Time passed and it was in 1963 at the time of the big freeze that Don went ice skating on Bolder Mere near Wisley. One of his neighbours with whom he had become quite friendly said he was off skating and wondered if Don would like to go. The lake was frozen solid and Don found his old skates he had used in Canada and off they went skating for two or three hours. It was the same Christmas that he had brought his mother over to stay for a few days and she ended up staying until the second week in February because of the snow blocking roads.

The following year the company asked him to go to Holland to work with their agents over there. So he flew to Amsterdam and was driven out to S'Hertogenbosch. He stayed a few days working with a Dutch colleague and then was invited to go to an electro-plating exhibition in Utrecht where the agent had a stand. At Utrecht he was royally entertained and then the agent asked his secretary to take him to Amsterdam and show him around. In the city he was given a first-class lunch in a very smart restaurant and then taken by the young secretary on a tour of the city before finally taking him to Schipol airport for his return to the UK. When he got back home from Holland he was greeted with the sad news that his friend, who he had gone skating with the year before, had been killed in a car crash near home and had already been buried.

For holiday this year they decided to drive down to Devon and take pot luck on accommodation.

They got down to Teignmouth and were crossing the bridge over the river when the car stopped. The engine had blown a gasket, although the car had been serviced just a day before leaving, obviously the mechanic had not tightened the gasket properly. They managed to get the car towed to a garage but being Bank Holiday weekend there was no one available to do the repair, so the only thing was to find somewhere to stay over the weekend. They found a bed and breakfast nearby and spent the rest of the weekend driving around the Teignmouth area. Young Stephen was not at all happy with the B&B but never said so at the time although years later he confessed as much.

Whilst in Teignmouth they thought about looking for a small house or bungalow to buy as a second home, but eventually gave up trying having only seen one within their budget but not quite what they were looking for. However, the seed had been sown and a second home near the sea occupied their thoughts. They continued to consider it and finally later that year decided that perhaps a static caravan would fit the bill and having found a site near Weymouth that seemed to be suitable went ahead and bought one. Their first holiday in a caravan the following year proved to be a big success, being particularly enjoyed by young Stephen who was able to roam around the camp and up the hills at the side of the caravan park.

At work Don was asked to go to France with one of the senior chemists. The company were considering making an investment in a French company in Grenoble who had a plant using a new procedure of painting electro-statically. The people were quite friendly and took Don and his colleague up in the mountains to a very high-class restaurant. All the menu was of course in French and Don not remembering a great deal of French from his school days could only recognise one word in the choice for the main course which he thought must be pork, so he chose it. It was obvious from the reaction of the French present that they considered him to be a gourmet, no one else chose this. It turned out to be wild boar and did not at all suit his palate. He did manage to swallow it, but thought it awful and of course had to pretend he enjoyed it. They stayed two nights in Grenoble and then travelled by train to Paris to look at the small branch factory of the Grenoble company. There Don had his first experience of meeting French factory workers and going with them to a small café. He would always remember how one of the men became the centre of attention as he was the only one who had been to England; when asked where he had been he said it was to Jersey. The question of buying the French company, however, fell through.

The years rolled on and by 1967 Stephen had taken the eleven plus, passed, and was now attending the Woking Grammar School.

Don had made many improvements in procedures at work and very soon he was made a director and appointed to the board of his company, the company making the biggest profit contribution to the Group. He had already been given a company car some months earlier.

Betty was always very close to her family, including the many aunts and uncles living in and around Edmonton and they knew that Don was doing well and thus it came as no surprise when Betty's uncle Ted, who lived near the family home in Edmonton, asked Don whether he would mind being a referee for a job he had applied for at Barclays Bank, he having lost his previous job in the city through no fault of his own. Don of course was happy to do so and wrote a letter to the bank which obviously helped as Ted wrote a very kind letter back, when he got the job, thanking him for his help. It was not long after this that he was asked if he could help find a position for their son David who had just finished at university having obtained a degree in Chemistry. Don asked the manager in charge of the chemical division of the company if he could use a newly qualified chemist and David came along for an interview and was taken on in the laboratories. David found digs in Woking and one night a week was entertained for dinner at Don's house staying overnight. David got on well working in the laboratory and visiting customers but after a few months decided it was not for him, applied for another job and left.

Chapter Thirty-Four

Time went by and one day Don's good friend Eric, a man who had been with the company longer and who was also a director, came into his office and shocked Don by asking if he would go to Moscow to negotiate a contract with the Russians. Eric, who was a salesman, had a couple of years before taken a Land Rover, fitted with samples of the company's products, over to Europe and driven all the way to Moscow and attended an exhibition. Since then interest had been shown in what the company could do and finally they were asked to quote to supply plating machinery for the Moscovitch car. Being their first quotation they had hardly expected it to be considered but it had happened and they were not confident that they would be competent to negotiate, having heard terrible stories of companies losing their shirts when dealing with the Russians.

Don undoubtedly was held in high regard by the senior directors of the Group and they had decided that the best person to go to Moscow for this job would be him. He had been taken completely by surprise as he had never dreamed he would be asked to negotiate with the Russians even though, as written above, in one of his first years with the company he had successfully tied up a contract in London with a very large Japanese company; but going to Moscow was different. It was a time when the Cold War was at its height, Russia was an unknown quantity for most; no one he knew, or indeed his friends and relations outside the company he knew, had known anyone who had been there; the country had been virtually closed for years. But as said above, one of the company's directors had taken the plunge and had managed to get the Russians interested. When interest was shown in the company's quotation they had sent a young chemist/salesman to further things along. Although it could not be said the Soviet Union was opening up, it had been reported that there were representatives from other countries showing interest in the contract. The young chemist said he knew that Germans, French and Italians were also trying to sell themselves to the Russians.

Betty was certainly taken aback when he told her the company wanted him to go to Russia and not a little worried. He told her he would be meeting the company sales representative out there and that other staff members had been there and returned quite safely, although he knew that no one particularly liked the experience and much preferred to go to Poland, where several inroads had already been made, and where there were far less restrictions and one was not being watched all the time.

Over the next few weeks he had to make a number of visits up to London to liaise with the company's bankers and ECGD (Export Credit Guarantees department). The latter because it was almost certain the Russians would want credit and it was very necessary to find out exactly what was required in a contract by the British government before granting credit. Eventually the flight was arranged and just a day before he was due to go the company received a message from their representative in Moscow to say the Russians were not quite ready and it was necessary for the flight to be delayed for a few days. The message added a footnote saying, 'Would you please get Don to bring an electric kettle as they would like one at the Embassy.'

So the kettle was bought and at the same time Eric suggested that it would be a good idea to get a few ball point pens to hand out as they were scarce out there and he also handed over two gold pens to give to the senior Russians. "What do I do about declaring them?" Don asked. "Oh just say nothing, you'll be all right." Don resolved then and there to make a proper declaration as he had no desire to end up in the Lubyanka.

A few days later he boarded a Comet aircraft at London, Heathrow, and flew to Moscow. He passed through customs, declaring the kettle and pens and was met by the company sales representative, Terry Winter, outside the airport. Terry then went over to the Intourist guide and found out which hotel Don had been allocated.

"You're booked in at the Metropole," Terry said.

"Is that where you are?"

"No, I am at the Leningradskaya. I guess they do this to unsettle one or something. I'll never understand why."

They took a taxi into Moscow and having seen Don in to his hotel, Terry left and said he would come around later that evening and they would go out to dinner with a Russian friend who had been of help to him.

Dinner was at an Uzbekistan restaurant and Don and his small party were ushered in and to a table, all in front of the queue of Russians who were obliged to wait while it seemed Intourist people went ahead. The meal over, Terry said he would be around to Don's hotel in the morning when they would go off to the Ministry of Foreign Trade.

The following morning they went down into the underground at a station near the hotel and on to the station close to the offices they were to attend. Terry gave the appropriate words to the guard outside and they were allowed in where after waiting a short while they were met by two Russians who took them up in the lift to the office where they were to begin discussions on the contract.

Terry had told Don that he had built up his reputation and told the Russians that he was a very important man. Don was not sure whether to be pleased about this but since it had been done he had to accept it. The Russians spoke English and the negotiations began, three Russians facing the two Englishmen. The first considerations was the price and it immediately became clear that they expected a big discount which Don had been prepared for but which he knew, since he had asked before leaving England, was going to be purely guesswork as no one at home seemed to have any idea how much, if anything, had been built in the price and available to give away.

The negotiations went on all day and finally they shook hands with a discount of fifteen per cent. Following this they were given the contract they were supposed to sign the following day. The contract consisted of about fifty pages of clauses, written in English, which over the next three weeks Don and Terry were to become very familiar. That evening they spent time in Don's room reading through and amending as was thought necessary.

Over the next three weeks there were daily visits, except Sundays, to the Ministry of Foreign Trade building and the negotiations continued, the final agreed contract bearing little resemblance to the original handed to Don and his colleague. The Russians said they would like the amended contract retyped but as they had not a suitable English typewriter available at that time they asked them to arrange this. Don and Terry left the building feeling very pleased with themselves, Don in particular as he knew he had negotiated a fair contract and managed to get all the ECGD requirements included which was not easy. How to get the contract typed, Terry thought, would not be difficult as the Embassy owed them a favour for bringing the kettle over, so off they went with the draft for typing.

It had, however, not been all work in Moscow as Terry had before Don's arrival booked seats for a concert at the Moscow Conservatoire where they had a truly memorable Beethoven evening including, 'The Egmont', 'The Pastoral' and the 'Emperor Piano Concerto'. Then on one Sunday they had been taken out into the country by an obviously well-respected Russian Professor from the Mendaliav Institute, who was interested in their company's work. They had been driven out from Moscow to the limit allowed for foreigners, the professor bringing along his wife and daughter. Terry and Don on another evening entertained the man and his wife to dinner in Metropole hotel.

The Commercial Section of the British Embassy was a place where in an evening British in Moscow could spend some time talking and getting light refreshments. It was also the place where the kettle Don had brought over with him had found a home. It was therefore the place Terry was sure he could get someone to retype the contract. However, when they arrived at the Embassy everyone appeared to be in a panic and it was difficult to get anyone to speak to them. When they did eventually get someone to listen they were told there was not a hope of getting the contract typed as Embassy staff were preparing to leave for London on the return flight of the Comet that had just brought the Foreign Secretary, George Brown, over for discussions in Moscow brought about by the heightening crisis in the Middle East. It seemed employees and their families were all preparing to leave, it was almost as if they were expecting something dreadful to happen. Thus Don and his colleague were thwarted but Terry was a very resourceful person and he immediately thought of an Australian girl he knew who worked at the Australian Embassy. However, when he managed to get in touch with her he found she was too busy to contemplate undertaking such work. She realised however that they were in a desperate position and said she had an Australian friend staying with her for a few days travelling to London via Moscow and this lady could type and might be prepared to do it using the typewriter in the flat.

Eventually Terry was given instructions to go to the flat as his friend had said she would look at what was required and might be willing to do their typing. They arrived at the flat the following morning and found the young lady in a dressing gown having just jumped out of bed.

She examined the contract and was a little shocked to find it was much longer than she had anticipated when her friend had told her about it.

"We will pay you, of course," Don said. "Tell us how much you think it is worth?"

The young lady thought for a moment and asked if she could be paid in pounds Sterling as she was going on to London.

"It would be nice if you could arrange for the payment to be waiting for me to draw at the overseas club in London."

"Yes I can arrange that. Will £10 be OK?"

The young lady was obviously well pleased and said she would do her best to get the contract typed that day. For his part Don sent a telex to his MD asking for £10 to be sent to the overseas club in London to be collected by Miss Jones from Australia; he wickedly added 'for services rendered', knowing this would cause a laugh.

They collected the typed contract the next day and took it with them to the Ministry building. They were met by the same people and taken to the room where the negotiations had taken place and where they expected to sign the contract. The two Englishmen said afterwards that they noticed the Russians seemed to be ill at ease and somewhat tense.

"Please sit down."

"We have had the contract typed and it is already to sign. We have two copies."

"I am sorry we cannot sign, our client has just told us they have not the money to pay."

The senior Russian spoke and again repeated he was sorry. Don was taken aback, they had been three weeks negotiating and everything was ready for signature and now the Russians were claiming their client, supposedly Moscovitch, was not supposed to have any money to pay and they were getting ECGD credit for most of it. Don did not want to go back to England with nothing and thought hard.

"Could you give us a Letter of Intent?" he asked.

The senior Russian thought for a moment and then said he would find out whether this was possible. He left the office for nearly half an hour and then came back to say it would be possible and that he had arranged for this to be typed and given to them. Don was very relieved, although he knew that a Letter of Intent was not legally binding. Some ten minutes later the letter arrived in the office, Don read it and said it was satisfactory. They shook hands with the Russians and left. There was nothing to do now but arrange for a flight back to the UK. However, Terry, who had travelled a lot over Europe in his capacity as a salesman, said they deserved a night in Copenhagen and that the only extra cost would be the hotel. It seems he had taken this particular route home before.

There was the usual close inspection at the airport and before boarding the plane soldiers stopped all passengers at the steps and went into the plane and it seemed carefully examined the aircraft for possible bombs, something that outside the Soviet Union was never practised at that time, but which today would not be thought to be excessive. It was because of the feeling of always being followed and worrying what might happen that much later on one or two engineers working for Don's company would refuse to go back there again. However, it had not bothered Don and his colleague.

They found an hotel in Copenhagen and in the evening after walking around the town went along to the Tivoli Gardens, the famous entertainment centre. They returned to Heathrow the following morning and duly reported back to the company. Don told the MD and other assembled directors that they had not got an order but had managed to get a Letter of Intent. The MD and others congratulated them and were elated with having such an undertaking even though Don had pointed out that the letter had no force in law. It was obvious they assumed they had as good as got an order. However, the tension in the Middle East remained, with the Soviet Union supporting the Arabs and Britain supporting the Israelis. A few days later the Six Day War happened.

The year wore on and in late summer Don arranged to take the family down to their caravan, and it was whilst there late one night on returning from a long drive to North Devon, Don on opening the door of the caravan immediately spotted something on the floor that looked like a telegram. He opened it, it was indeed a telegram, and found that the MD wanted him to return the following day, if possible, as 'the Russians were coming'.

He set his alarm for early the next morning and was off to Surrey by five o'clock and arrived home, changed into office clothes and was at the office by nine o'clock. The MD was obviously relieved and pleased to see him as he made it clear they would have been at a loss as to what to do when the Russians arrived.

The Russians arrived at ten o'clock and Don was pleased to see he knew all three men, two of whom had been present right through the negotiations. Sitting in the Board Room the meeting got under way with the MD and Eric, the director who had asked him to go to Moscow, present. There were certain things the Russians wanted changed in the contract, two copies of which they put on the table. Don, who had his own copy of the contract, asked what they were. The changes suggested were relatively minor and Don made appropriate alterations to the Russian's satisfaction. However, they wanted to go through the whole contract again and thus the meeting continued longer than seemed initially to be necessary. Having finally agreed it was then necessary for each page of both contracts to be initialled by both parties and thus Don and his opposite number continued to do this whilst others at the meeting talked. There were final discussions on the agreed implementation of the contract and the meeting finally came to an end near to midnight. The meeting had lasted many hours but the Russians did not want to break for any meal and only sandwiches and coffee were consumed.

As the meeting was breaking up, Eric suggested they all went round to his house for a celebration party and a few drinks. However, Don, who was strictly on holiday, asked the Russians to excuse him explaining he had come back from holiday purposely to meet them and that he had to return to his family in the West Country. They embraced him and thanked him and hoped to see him again next time he came to Moscow. The MD called Don into his office before he left for the party with the others and thanked him for all he had done for the company. He then proceeded to tell him that he had been talking to the Group MD, both of whom were shortly due to retire, and they had agreed to advise the Board to appoint Don as the next Group Chief Executive and that they would get him elected to the main Board at the next meeting. Don was of course overwhelmed and could not wait to tell Betty the news. He drove home and went to bed for a few hours before setting off early to drive down to Dorset.

He was duly appointed to the main Board but somehow felt guilty, or at least slightly embarrassed, as he had gone ahead of the Group Company Secretary, a very well-respected man, who Don looked upon as much senior to him, and who not only efficiently ran everything for the Group and of course had for years attended all Group Board meetings, but was the very man who had employed him as a junior assistant accountant a few years earlier. Don had not changed but his progress in the company had been nothing short of a miracle.

The receipt of the contract was headline news in the local paper and a number of people he knew stopped him in the street and congratulated him. It was suggested by his neighbour that he should give some talks as many people would be interested to know all about being in Russia at that time. Don said he was too busy, a rather lame excuse.

Chapter Thirty-Five

Having succeeded on one contract he was not surprised when later that year he was asked if he would negotiate another contract plus a possible one for another subsidiary in the Group, one closely associated with his company. These contracts with the Russians were to be negotiated in Turin, Italy. The Russians were buying a complete factory for the manufacture of motor cars and had chosen the Italian giant Fiat. The plant was to be built in a town some five hundred miles from Moscow which would be renamed Togliatti after an apparently well-known Italian communist.

At home Betty and Don, now with a much improved income, had decided earlier that year they would like a better house and when Don spotted an advertisement for a new house to be built in a road nearer to West Byfleet he went along to see and met the agent and builder, the latter wanting stage payments. So Don bought the land and signed a contract for the payments to be made. They decided they would like a games room added with a terrace above it with access from the main bedroom, and this was therefore included in the price. It was a four-bedroom house and was advertised as £11,500 and with the additional room it was then to be £12,300. It was going to be near to Christmas 1967 when they would be able to move. Their first house with three bedrooms and central heating was put up for sale for £8,000. (These houses in 1968 are put on the market for say £450,000 today.) The houses being built when they had first moved down to Surrey did not have central heating which became popular several years later, about the time of North Sea Gas arriving, but Don had, with guidance of two engineers in his company, installed it himself but on his own admission, although it worked, it was not a very professional job.

With respect to the forthcoming Russian contracts he had to go through the same procedure in London as he had for the Moscovitch contract but the second time around was easier, he knew what their bank and ECGD required and within two weeks he was ready to go for the first one, an exceptionally large contract which if successfully negotiated would have to be built in a shipyard down in Southampton. He flew on a BEA Trident and took a taxi to the Hotel Ambasciatori in mid-town Turin. There he met Eric who would be helping with any technical negotiations, all of which would be taking place at offices in the Piazza San Carlo where the Russians had taken over a building.

The first meeting was held the following morning and the two Englishmen were met at the entrance by a doorkeeper who telephoned through to the appropriate person whilst asking the visitors to be seated. Shortly, two Russians came out of a lift and introduced themselves. Don was pleased to see that one was the senior he had dealt with both in Moscow and back in the office when they had returned to sign the earlier contract. The four men went up in the lift and into an office where after pleasantries the negotiations on price started. After some three hours they agreed a price and were handed the contract which of course the Russians wanted them to sign.

"It is the standard contract, look at it for a while and we will sign, yes?"

"Now come on, comrade, you know we will not do that, we will have to take it away to study and meet you again. You know that as your client will almost certainly want credit, we are bound to include those clauses I had put in when we met in Moscow on the Moscovitch contract. This contract has got to be the same," Don said.

"Ah you know we have to try to get it settled with as little delay as possible, we can but try. You are a hard man," he said smiling, "We meet tomorrow at ten."

Over the next several days the negotiations continued but headway was slow. Twice Don found it necessary to return to London to clear matters with ECGD as the Russians were being difficult and wanted to make changes to the credit requirements. On the last visit it was suggested that he return with a solicitor, appointed with the blessing of ECGD, to add weight to the arguments put forward. It was also agreed that a secretary should be sent to Turin to help with the paperwork and particularly the anticipated final typing of the contract. The secretary proved to be an attractive young lady wearing the new fashion mini skirt, common enough in England at the time but which had not yet reached Italy. She caused a sensation in the hotel and outside in the streets and sought Don's 'protection' as she claimed she been chased around her room by a member of the hotel staff. She came along to the meetings with the young solicitor as she felt safer there than being left alone in the hotel.

Back at home the move to the new house arrived and poor Betty had to arrange everything for the move to take place. Don, on one of his visits back from Turin, found the move had gone successfully and that Betty had done a good job. The removal company charged £15.10s.0d.

Towards the end of the negotiations in Turin, the Russians brought in their big guns, none other than the vice president of AvtopromImport. This man was really tough and made it clear that he wanted to get the contract finished that day. He spoke English with a strong deep accent, his first words were, "We agree a clause and we drink. Yes?" and he meant it. The first clause was agreed and on orders from the vice president the waiter poured everyone Vodka, the vice president stood up, everyone followed, and with a suitable word he swallowed the drink and everyone did the same. Don felt they should have then all thrown their glasses in the fireplace, and would have done if the vice president had done so. However, he sat down and urged the senior comrade to get on to the next clause, and so the day rolled on with the noise in the room gradually increasing. The young solicitor began to look decidedly green, and the waiter noticing this hardly poured any drink in his glass although making out as if he had done so. The clauses seemed endless and night drew on. Also present was a Russian lawyer, who it seemed from the card given to Don was the top government lawyer for the Soviet Union. It was his task, with Don's help, to rewrite clauses suitable to both parties and it became increasingly difficult as the noise increased and the drinks continued to flow. The young female secretary had been sent back to the hotel in the afternoon, Don arranging for her to be escorted there by a technical colleague familiar with the contract, who was staying at the hotel. He had been brought over to Turin in case awkward technical questions were asked on the plant to be supplied.

It was near to midnight when the last clause was agreed.

"We will meet tomorrow at ten to sign? Yes?"

That morning in the hotel Don hurriedly wrote down his version of what had happened the night before and at breakfast showed it to Eric who after reading said, "You should write a book."

At the meeting that morning Don and the senior Russian negotiator initialled each page of the two copies of the contract and finally it was signed by two Russians and the two Englishmen. It was by far the largest contract the company had ever quoted for and as stated above would have to be built in a shipyard.

Back home the local press got hold of the story and once again splashed it as headlines in the local paper. The order was worth £2.3 million and this before the rampant inflation a few years ahead meaning that at the beginning of the twenty-first century a comparable figure would be nearer £100 million. Thus he had now successfully negotiated two Russian contracts.

After Christmas he was again approached by the MD and asked if he would negotiate the other possible Russian contract, this time for the associated subsidiary company, fifty per cent owned by an American company. The previous contracts had been for supplying machinery to be used in the motor car industry for metal plating and this new one was again for the motor industry but this time instead of plating machinery it was for metal polishing machinery. The contract was substantial, in excess of a million, although not quite so big as the last one. He would be working with two men he knew well, Al Curle. the MD of the subsidiary and Roy Canfield their Sales Manager, both very good sorts.

In case the reader may think that to obtain the contract one had to simply negotiate price and wording of clauses, it is as well to know that other country representatives were present in Turin, often in the same hotel, working to get those contracts for themselves. Of course the quality of the machinery had to be first rate but one has to assume that the Russians had already done their homework and would not be wasting time talking to countries whose equipment was sub standard, thus the Germans, French and Italians present were all in the running and the same had been the situation with the previous successful negotiations.

The negotiations started towards the end of April and the price was agreed on the first day. Then there was a period when one assumes negotiations were taking place with the competition and thus it was two days before they were called again to the Piazza San Carlo. It seemed they could well have been the chosen one but nothing was said to this effect. At the end of this meeting Don and his colleagues were told the offices would be closed the next day as it was 1st May and holiday for Russians. At that time Britain had no holiday on this day, however, the English negotiating party decided to treat it as a holiday also and so they ordered a car for the following day so they could drive over the Alps to Monte Carlo.

The following morning, Roy, the sales manager, the appointed driver, successfully managed the mountain roads and they duly arrived in Monte Carlo in time for lunch. They spent

193

an enjoyable day looking around the place and before leaving for Turin, Roy drove the car through the famous tunnel that features in the Formula 1 annual motor car race.

Another two days and all the clauses in the contract had been agreed when a telex arrived at their hotel to say the German Mark had been revalued. Unfortunately, there was in the contract a substantial piece of equipment to be built in Germany and Don knew there could well be complications which would affect the price the company had agreed. He therefore told the Russians he was not prepared to sign until he had been back to London to check the position. For their part the Russians said they wanted to sign the contract and had arranged for the President of AvtopromImport to come later that evening to sign on their behalf. Don said he could not sign until the cost for the German element in the contract had been cleared. The senior Russian obviously thought Don would sign now he knew such an important person was coming in to meet them and sign.

"Let us initial the pages and you come back later and you will sign. Yes?"

Don said he was happy to initial and repeated that he could not sign.

"Come back at eleven tonight. Mt Butko will be coming straight from an important dinner to meet you. You will sign."

Don, however, booked his flight home and joined the others late that night in the Russian's office. Near to midnight the president arrived and was obviously quite put out to learn that Don would not sign, particularly after he had come along to the meeting so late at night. The senior Russian negotiator was obviously embarrassed as he was sure Don would buckle under and sign with such an important man present. Don apologised but said, "It is more than my job's worth to sign without clearing the financial situation with respect to the Mark."

He returned to London and after talking to his MD bought German Marks forward to be sure that no other changes would affect the position. He returned to Turin, told the Russians that he had sorted out the problem and was ready to sign. They arranged for him to meet the president the next day and the contract was signed. Don sensed that the president respected him for his firm stand and signed, shaking hands warmly.

Chapter Thirty-Six

A few months later a Group cocktail party was arranged and Don and Betty were invited and much to Don's surprise he and his wife were introduced to the guests present as the next Group Chief Executive and his wife. The happy position Don was in was, however, not to last very long as a series of events were to take all this away.

However, there was one event at this time that stood out. It was decided that the company would try and get the Russian Ambassador in London to come to a small dinner at the Savoy. They told the embassy that it would just be a small party but they would like him and his wife to join two directors and their wives for dinner. The ambassador accepted the invitation knowing the company was working with the Soviets on three big contracts. It was agreed that Don and Eric, to be accompanied by their wives, be the two directors to attend the dinner. Don went along with Betty to buy a new dress and all was set for the dinner to take place. The booking had been made at the Savoy including, as the Embassy had told them, booking a table for KGB men who were required to be present. This done everything was now ready for the dinner, but when quite suddenly the Soviet government expelled twenty or so British diplomats from Moscow, the British retaliating by sending an equal number of Russians back from London to Moscow, everything went pear-shaped and shortly after the company had a telephone call to say it was not possible for the Ambassador to be seen in public dining with British and so the dinner was cancelled. However, the company, not to be outdone, decided to see whether the ambassador would be prepared to attend a cocktail party in a private suite in the same hotel. He agreed and thus preparations were made for another evening at the Savoy.

Apart from certain members of staff who were directly or indirectly involved in the Russian contracts, the company invited a number of important people involved in the export business, including a number of Russians from the Soviet Commercial offices in Highgate and also several Polish diplomatic and commercial representatives. Then there were added several important people such as the chairman of the East European Trade Council, representatives at senior level from ECGD, an MP who was a former Minister of State from the Board of Trade, bank managers, accountants etc. This was all listed internally and staff allocated to look after important people. The list arrived on Don's desk and he was shocked to see he had been allocated the top two men – the Russian Ambassador and the Chairman of the East European Trade Council. He of course was the senior employee attending the meeting but had hoped that someone better equipped than him at socialising would have been chosen.

However, he said nothing and kept his inward fears to himself. The evening arrived and he and Eric plus one other boarded a Rolls Royce and drove to the Savoy. They purposely arrived early, well before guests were due to arrive and Don immediately set about preparing himself for meeting the Ambassador by drinking Champagne. In fact he sank six glasses and felt decidedly better and quite prepared to meet anybody. The guests duly arrived and Don met the Ambassador and introduced him to other senior people present. Don got along well with the man and very soon was going round asking people if they would like to meet the Russian Ambassador. Of course they all wanted to and he duly took them along one by one to meet him. The evening was a great success and everyone seemed to enjoy themselves, the drinks of course flowed and the snacks, smoked salmon and others were always available from the many waiters that the hotel supplied. One Russian who he had met in Moscow tried to talk him into doing a little industrial espionage but of course he declined. The Ambassador thanked Don and others for a lovely evening and it was over.

A few days later the company received an unexpected telephone call from the then Prime Minister, Harold Wilson, thanking the company for 'breaking the ice' with the Russians.

As was said above, the happy position Don was in did not last as soon the American company from whom the licence to sell chemicals had some years before been obtained (chemicals manufactured by the company with which Don had been mostly associated), asked if they could buy a stake in the Group. The Board readily accepted the proposal, particularly as the people in that company were well known to certain members of the Board and had been friends with them for many years. Thus steps were taken to allow some of the Board members to sell shares up to the amount the Americans had asked for. Everything was going well when suddenly the Group were told by the Americans that they had to stop as their own company had quite out of the blue become the victim of a takeover by a huge American Chemical Company.

Very shortly after the aborted sale of shares, Don's Group had an offer from this giant American Chemical Corporation to buy all the shares. The president of that company came over to England and talks were held and the sale was verbally agreed and the Group would continue as hitherto but of course the whole company would become a subsidiary of the American company. The president seemed to be a man they could trust and it was agreed therefore that the Board would recommend the shareholders to sell their shares at the very favourable price offered. However, whilst the president was present in the Group's Head Office a telex was received for his attention. It stated that negotiations must cease as an American oil company, Occidental Petroleum, was about to buy the giant chemical company. The president therefore returned to America and soon after the representatives of the oil company came to the Head Office of the Group.

One could see right away that these people were a different kettle of fish. However, at a Board meeting only one director thought the takeover should not be allowed to happen; he, however, crumbled when he and the Group MD met the oil men in a private meeting. It seemed the price was too good to miss, plus the golden handshakes offered to directors who were due to retire. Thus Don's company was taken over and very soon they learnt they were to report to a small company in Switzerland.

Meanwhile at home Betty had become ill and Don paid for her to have an operation in a private hospital. However, he had been warned when she had been in a mental hospital after their son was born, that any shock to the system might trigger a return to the same state of depression and sadly this is precisely what happened. Betty recovered from the operation but became depressed and had to be taken to a local mental hospital where she was kept in and given, once again, the terrible shock treatment used at that time. Don visited her most evenings and at the weekends; it was a very trying time for them. She seemed to get a good deal better, particularly when several of her family came along to the hospital one weekend. Eventually she was allowed home but was to return regularly for treatment.

The first meeting with representatives of the Swiss subsidiary showed at once what the Americans wanted to do. The representative, who claimed he had been educated at the Sorbonne, explained a method of avoiding taxation which the American company wished to adopt. They wanted the British company, heavily into export, to change its method of charging for goods sent overseas. Instead of invoicing the customer or agent as hitherto, they wanted the price charged on invoices to be drastically cut, in fact everything to be only very little above cost, but instead of invoices being made to the customer the invoices should be sent to the Swiss company who then would invoice the true invoice price to the customer. Thus profits from the operation were to be transferred to the Swiss company. Since one of the companies in the group, the one Don had first worked for, had successfully lived for some years with big mark-ups on the chemicals it sold, such a move would mean the company would begin to make a loss whilst the profits available were transferred to the Swiss company as apparently there were more favourable arrangements with America.

Don spoke up at the meeting, saying that this was contrary to the Companies Acts and the conditions that the Americans had been given permission by HM government to buy the company. Undoubtedly this objection was noted by the new bosses but it made no difference, they intended to go ahead and knew it would be a big undertaking for anyone to change it.

All the main board directors except one were given golden handshakes and retired. The one they held on to was Don, the Financial Director, and they obviously thought he could be of use to them over the next period. There was now no Managing Director or Chief Executive of the Group and the Swiss company on instructions from America were told to form a committee to run the Group. They had of course been told that the next Chief Executive on retirement of the most senior directors was to have been Don and so they made him Chairman of the committee with a grandiose title of United Kingdom Occidental Coordinator of Finance and Administration.

He found that the requirements for reporting monthly to America necessitated an increase in workload on the Accounts department to such an extent that initially there was much overtime until additional staff could be found. Now committees are no way to run a company, it just does not work, and Don reported to the Swiss representative that things were beginning to go wrong, each person on the committee wanting to do things their own way. He sensed this was what they expected to happen and they then agreed to appoint a man to be managing director. They said they would decide this by taking four people to the Alps for a review session. The four were made up of three from the Group and a new man transferred from the Swiss company. Thus Don went along with the others to Megeve where the first meetings, attended by representatives of the Swiss company, became sessions in which each member had to state why he should be the new MD and why he was better than any of the others. It was quite distasteful and Don found it difficult to go along with it. On another day the four were taken to the top of a mountain and given ski bobs and told to ride down to the bottom. Not properly clothed and simply, in Don's case, in the overcoat he had used from home, they started off down the mountainside. Don, his first time on such a contraption and never having skied, kept up with the Swiss rep who was going to make the choice, himself a lifetime skier and used to the Alps, and when the Swiss in front fell, Don landed on top of him, which Don said afterwards couldn't have done much to help his cause.

At about twelve that night the Swiss rep came along to tell the three group candidates that it had been decided to appoint the fourth member to be MD. It was probably inevitable but what surprised the Sorbonne man was that the three group representatives said they would not accept the decision. A frantic phone call must then have been made to America and the decision changed to appoint Don's friend, Eric, as the man for the job, whilst their man would become deputy. Returning to the UK the new situation caused some concern but had to be accepted.

Don still had the best office in the building, the one previously vacated by the Group Managing Director. Eric as the new MD was clearly concerned that Don, who he had much respect for and who he knew was disappointed not to be given the top job as promised before the takeover, would seek employment elsewhere, indeed he knew that prior to the takeover Don had been head-hunted by a number of companies in industry. Eric therefore tried to think of a way not to lose him and hit upon the idea of seeing that he had an improved company car and he therefore ordered a Daimler Sovereign and having got the garage to get it ready for collection told Don what he had done. At the time Don, although disappointed at what had been done had no intention of changing employment at a time when Betty was so unwell as he knew it would be too much of a worry when she was receiving treatment at a mental hospital. So Don simply collected his new super car, an automatic.

Chapter Thirty-Seven

Some months went by and Eric was inevitably 'promoted' to a position in Geneva and in his place, the Swiss newcomer, became MD, the one who the owners had wanted to appoint in Megeve. After a few months they had cleverly got their way. Don did not like this man, a slimy individual, well in with the American owners, helped no doubt by the fact that he too was Jewish. Don suspected the feeling was mutual but he knew that for the time being he was key to the company and without his support things might not go so well. However, if Betty had not been unwell he would undoubtedly have looked for employment elsewhere.

Gradually the accounts department got on top of reporting and the new MD began to understand the workings of the group. He was a man who, in Don's and many others' opinion, if he had been employed in the group before takeover might have made his way to a secondary management position but certainly not to the exalted position of Chief Executive and a member of the main board.

Betty left hospital after a few weeks but had to return two or three times each week for treatment. It became awkward for Don but his secretary volunteered to take her and fetch her back on those occasions when it became too difficult to get time.

It was during this difficult period that information came to hand of a very big Russian contract that the new group would like to try for. The contract was for a vast lorry plant to be built in a town near the Kama River and thus it was known as the Kama River project. It was necessary, as the contract was so big, for a team to be appointed to manage the various aspects for preparation of a quotation. It was decided unanimously that

Don should chair the team formed and that he appoint a deputy. He chose an old friend of his who had worked with him in Italy and on various other jobs. He got Joe to get representatives from all the departments that would be involved and a first meeting was held and the contract proposals from the Russians aired. It became clear that many months would be needed to put together a suitable quotation and each department was allocated work to do and it was agreed that regular meetings every two weeks be held to examine progress, with the option to call a special meeting if difficulties were encountered that it was necessary to overcome in the short term.

It was now nearly three years since the takeover and it had become clear that the Americans were not happy with some of the results they were getting from the British company. Don was called to a meeting with the American corporation president, a man who had made millions from his enterprise, in particular from oil. Don had not met him previously but his reputation was well known and it was said by Americans in the company that one got a gold medal if you stayed in the company for three years but that they did not know of any who had lasted that long. The man was the son of a Jewish immigrant to the USA from Russia. He was in his eighties; had already retired when he bought a small oil company which he had built to be one of the biggest in the world. Having taken all he could from oil he had then moved into other fields, such as chemicals, and had continued to expand the corporation. He was staying in Claridges in London.

Don duly met the man in his hotel suite and took an instant dislike to him. The man, Armand Hammer, soon made it clear that he was not happy with the figures produced by one side of the business that had been the personal field of the old Group Managing Director. This was an engineering division in which profits could be affected by the valuation placed on Work In Progress and there did not seem much doubt that the old MD had likely valued the WIP favourably when he negotiated a price for the shares in the group. Don pointed out that so many changes had been made and staff lost since the takeover that it was not surprising that profits were not as high. He also referred to the tax avoidance that had transferred most of the group's profits to the continent, a statement which the old man was obviously not too pleased to hear.

The initial meeting was just the two of them but near to lunch time the president said he was going to have his lunch and that they should meet at two when his solicitor would be present.

Don was angry that he had not been asked to share a lunch with him and had to leave the hotel and find somewhere to eat. It only confirmed what type of man this man was. Don bought a sandwich and sat in the nearby Green Park and watched the children playing on this bright and lovely summer day.

At the afternoon meeting with the solicitor present, Don did not say what he had thought about the possible valuation of WIP as he knew this was what the president wanted him to say. Nevertheless, it became obvious that the man was trying to build a case against the old MD who it seems must have outwitted this individual, a man always used to getting the better of people and grinding them into the ground.

Thus after the meeting Don contacted the ex MD and told him he would like to have a talk. A meeting was arranged for lunch at the MD's local golf course. Don told him what had happened at his meeting with the president and the old MD thanked him for what he had done.

A few weeks later on a Friday afternoon the MD of Don's company who had taken over from Eric put his head round the door of Don's office and said, "Could you come along and see me before you go tonight?"

Don said he would.

At about five o'clock he went along to the MD's office.

"You know I have been doing some reorganising."

"Yes, I did hear from Doug that something was happening but I was not told anything."

"Well, Don, we haven't a job for you in the new set-up. We are releasing you and giving you a year's salary and your car." He paused and then, "Would you like a drink?"

Don was taken completely by surprise; it was the last thing he had been expecting, and he was extremely angry at the way this individual, who he knew was not half the man he was, had so obviously undermined him.

"You can stuff your drink, Denis. I'll come in Monday and collect my cheque." Don walked out and slammed the door.

Going home he wondered how Betty would take the news. He drove up the drive of the new house they had moved to almost three years ago, parked the car and opened the front door where he was greeted by his wife.

"Betty I have some surprising news, they have sacked me. But don't worry I have a year's salary and my car, we will be all right."

As usual when Don came home tired and perhaps concerned, Betty said she would make a cup of tea and that her husband should sit in the armchair and she would put a record on to calm him down.

"Don't worry they'll regret doing it and we will get through," she said.

Stephen came in from school soon after and Don told him what had happened. He told him that there was nothing to worry about and that everything would be all right, "Dad's been given a year's salary and the Daimler is still ours."

Chapter Thirty-Eight

Unemployed

Don, however, was concerned and how easy it would be to get another job; at nearly fifty he was not so sure. The weekend passed and he arrived at the office to collect his cheque and the few personal belongings from his desk. The company secretary, who Don had appointed, came to see him and said he had been given instructions that he must sign his resignation or else he would not be able to hand over the cheque. Don signed but later wondered whether he had done the right thing, he left the office without saying goodbye to anyone.

From now on it was going to be necessary to try to find other employment. He started looking each day in the newspapers and here began the first of his letters of application sent together with a comprehensive CV that he straightway prepared; fortunately he had a portable typewriter which made things easier. It took a few days for the first replies to arrive and they were either a simple rejection or enclosed a very detailed form to be completed, more often than not almost exactly the same as the details already provided on his CV. He became accustomed to completing the forms and was soon opening the morning mail expecting either a new form or a rejection. It was not going to be easy. Three years earlier he had often been head-hunted but now things were different.

Betty was still unwell and Don had to take her regularly for treatment. Stephen seemed to be quite happy at school but whether he worried about his father's position Don never knew. Stephen, he knew, kept most things very much to himself.

The weeks passed and still not one single interview. It seemed strange that prior to the takeover companies or agents were ringing to try to get him to change his job but now it seemed no one wanted him. At first he applied for senior jobs, the same level as he had more recently become accustomed to, viz. financial directors, company secretaries, managing directors etc.

But as time went by he began to see that most were not interested as they probably wondered why he had been pushed out; surely, they probably thought, there must have been something wrong. So now the level of application was lowered and he succeeded in getting one or two interviews for assistant positions but at the interviews he sometimes saw that the person interviewing could easily have been worried after meeting him that his own position could be in jeopardy if he took this bright man on.

Christmas came and passed and he continued to send in applications which now numbered nearly fifty, but still no luck. Spring was no better and in summer he began to get very worried, Betty was only a little better and there seemed to be no light at the end of the tunnel. Then one day he remembered he had written quite a funny description of a meeting with Russians in Turin. He had written it on hotel paper before breakfast and showed it later to his friend Eric, who read it, laughed out loud and said, "You should write a book."

About this time he had a telephone call from Eric. Don was not surprised to hear that he too had been made redundant and he was ringing to ask advice as to what to do. The Americans' clever move 'promoting' him to a post in Geneva had only lasted so long and then they got rid of the one remaining senior employee of the old pre-takeover group. Eric decided eventually to go into business on his own and opened a small factory in the Midlands.

Don, who had some years before had one or two articles printed in business magazines, sent the short story to the editor of one of the magazines he knew. The man said he did not think he could print the story but said, "Why don't you write a book, you must have a lot to tell people and your style is very readable."

Don did not have to think about it for long, he talked to Betty and she too thought it a good idea, so he started. Over the next thirteen weeks he indeed wrote a book on his portable typewriter. Unlike writing today on a computer the only way of making alterations was by erasing typewriter fluid, and he also meticulously kept a carbon copy and typed on and on. Betty made him coffee in the mornings and tea in the afternoons and at each break he read what had been written. Betty seemed to like it and this encouraged him. The summer was hot and dry and whereas he should have been outside enjoying the garden or having a swim in the pool he and Stephen had built two years earlier, he continued to write and became completely absorbed in what he was writing. He finished the book at the end of thirteen weeks and throughout had kept a daily record of pages typed. The total was 525 pages, making the book nearly three inches thick, he called it *The Moscow Contract*.

Now what to do with it? He first sent it to the husband of Betty's wartime friend, Diana, who apparently had some connection with books, but exactly what Don never did find out. However, after several weeks he returned the book and had not had any success in getting it placed.

Don continued writing for jobs and even paid to see an agent who claimed to be able to help people to find work and give advice on what they should do. This was a bit of waste of money but seemed worth a try at the time.

He then had an interview with a small agency in Guildford who sent him to see a Jewish millionaire living in a big house in the Surrey hills. This man was very friendly; he wanted someone to look after his money and the estate. He was obviously impressed by Don, offered him the job and introduced him to his wife and hearing of Don's problems said he had no more need to worry any more as he would look after him. At lunch time Don rang Betty to tell her the good news.

That afternoon the man went out somewhere, leaving Don to talk to his wife with whom he had been told he would have to see quite a lot whilst working on the estate. Don and the lady got on very well – too well he wondered later? The man returned late in the afternoon and shortly after took Don to one side and told him he had changed his mind and that he did not want to employ him. Why he had retracted what he had said earlier Don had no idea – could he have rung what was left of his old company and talked to the Jewish owners? Don was shattered particularly as he had already told Betty he had the job. On leaving the house this man offered him one pound for his petrol money, Don did not accept and almost told him what he could do with it but refrained and left in a dignified manner. The man had told him that he was the cleverest man in England, he said he was the Vyella man who had invented the process. A real big-head. Don drove home carefully and broke the news to Betty.

A few weeks later he managed to get another interview for a senior position, this time with Duckham Oil at Crawley. The interview went well and he was invited back for a second meeting. It seemed he was one of two people and present at this interview was the Chairman, Lord........, the Managing Director and the Company Secretary. Don did not get the job but had the satisfaction of knowing that the Chairman had voted for him, as he told him afterwards, but was outvoted by the other two who thought the other man more suitable.

Chapter Thirty-Nine

Christmas arrived, the second since he had been unemployed, and he had a telephone call. It was a man who said he was the husband of Betty's doctor at the mental hospital. He said his wife had told him of the problem the husband of her patient was having finding work and wondered if he could be of help.

"I am a consultant and at the moment I have more work than I can possibly manage. I have a job down in Portsmouth which requires someone to go through all they do down there and look at all their systems and advise as necessary. Could you do this, do you think?"

Don was completely taken aback but managed to say that he thought he could and was very grateful to him for offering him the opportunity. If the man could have seen him he would have seen a tear rolling down his face but he hoped he never heard it in his voice. He was given instructions as to how to get to the factory and told that initially he would be given perhaps a week's work to test whether they thought him capable of doing the big job they wanted. Don thanked the man again and told Betty, who had been standing nearby, and had guessed there was some good news, and was anxious to know what it was all about.

Thus very early in the first week of the New Year Don set off for Portsmouth. The early morning train was a slow train and stopped at most stations along the line when later lots of school children crowded on, staying for a few stations before leaving. The station he was to go to, Hilsea, was just before Portsmouth and alighting he soon found the industrial estate and the factory he was to visit. He was first taken to the MD who told him what he expected him to do and said he would be paid for one week and in that time he should submit a report on what he recommended for improvements in the Accounting department.

He was introduced to the Accountant and it was not difficult to see that he was suspicious of this man coming in to check on his work. However, after the first day, the man was beginning to see that Don was quite a friendly person and that perhaps he did not pose a threat, and on the second day the man was convinced Don was only there to help. In his report at the end of the week Don gave the Accounts department a thumbs up and the MD, suitably impressed with the way the report had been presented, told him he would like him to go through every department in the offices and in the factory and produce for him a procedures manual with suitable recommendations for improvements.

The journey from West Byfleet to Hilsea continued all through January and the beginning of February. He had gone through administration, the drawing office, engineering, stores, and the various sections in the factory through to final assembly. The MD seemed pleased with his work and thanked him and said they would certainly employ him if, as was likely, a further study was envisaged.

Back at home his next-door neighbour learning of his short session in consultancy said he might be able to get him some work and a week or so later said he had a client in Hythe who needed some help. Don went down to see the company who built high-speed racing boats and after looking through their workshops and offices said there were several things he could do to improve the manufacturing process. They entertained him to an excellent lunch and said they would be in touch.

Don had recently written an article on takeovers which had been published in the magazine of one of his institutes and, after applying for a position with a company at present in Brixton but who had indicated they were shortly to move to Guildford, he was invited for interview. The interviewer turned out to be a member of the institute who had published Don's article and he had read it. Don was told he had been short listed and that they wanted him to come along for an interview with the partners. The position applied for was for Partnership Administrator of this international partnership of architects and engineers. Don met the partners and was offered the position, which he accepted.

It had been eighteen months since he had lost his last permanent employment and he had had to accept a salary considerably less than half that which he had been earning before. His wife was still unwell but during the time he had been at home there was no doubt she had improved but now he was to go to work every day and he was worried. He alerted her friends and a neighbour to try and keep an eye on her. Betty had been the secretary of the young wives institute at a church near Woking and so there were a number of ladies who knew her.

Chapter Forty

His new job was based in Brixton and thus he had to catch a train to Waterloo and then take the underground to Brixton. Although the hours were no more than was usual for offices at the time nevertheless it was quite late when he got home and obviously Betty missed him being at home. He looked forward to the office move to Guildford where he knew he could be home earlier.

He had started working for the partnership in April 1973 having left employment with the now American controlled company in October 1971 where he had started as assistant accountant in 1957. He had begun to get to grips with his work in Brixton and at first did not find it easy to accept that he now had several men who by their position as partners were senior to him, whereas in the position he had held just before he was made redundant most employees in the company were directly or indirectly responsible to him. He had reached his exalted position on his merits and he inwardly resolved that he would do his utmost to get there again.

To pass the time whilst travelling home from work he bought the *Evening Standard* at Waterloo station and one evening he read an article by Michael Booth, who as president of the Thomas Paine Society, wrote congratulating the author of the new biography of Thomas Paine. The author was Don's second cousin, Audrey Williamson, and he made his mind up to get the book and at the same time wondered whether he should write to her and see whether she could help him with the book he had written, *The Moscow Contract*.

Chapter Forty-One

Towards the end of June he noticed that Betty was occasionally more distant and sometimes sat as if she was deep in thought. He wished he had not always to leave her and again alerted friends about her.

In July Stephen was given the opportunity to go up to Scotland to the Open golf championship with Betty's friends, Thelma and Frank, who had moved up to live in Edinburgh as Frank's work had moved there. Frank was going to be a marshal at the Open and wondered if Stephen would like to come. He naturally jumped at the chance and duly went up to Scotland.

A day later Don walked home from West Byfleet station in the still bright sunlight. He walked up the drive and opened the door to his house and went inside. He called out to Betty but there was no reply. She must be in the garden or outside, he thought. His first instinct was to go upstairs and hurrying in the bedroom he saw Betty was in bed and asleep. He spotted a note on the bedside table picked it up and read, "Darling Don I must do this. Please forgive me. Betty." He tried to wake her but realised she was unconscious, he picked up the telephone and dialled 999 and asked for an ambulance. He then rushed next door to tell the neighbour what had happened, they of course were very sympathetic but could do nothing – he went back to the house and very soon the ambulance arrived. The ambulance men picked Betty up and put her on a stretcher and into the ambulance. They reassured Don that she would be all right and said he should follow in his car. It was impossible for him to keep up with the ambulance but when he arrived at the hospital he went to Accident and Emergency and they told him she was there. He was allowed to see her in a bed with a mask on her face and a young nurse sitting by her side. "Isn't the mask meant to be over her nose?" Don asked the nurse, who then hurriedly picked it up and placed it over Betty's nose. He was then told to go back into the waiting room where he stayed for several hours until they came out to tell him he might as well go home and return in the morning early. When he got home he telephoned her mother and told her what had happened.

The next morning he left home early at six o'clock and when he got to the hospital he was told there had been no change and that he could wait in the waiting room. An hour or so later, at a time when there were only one or two other people in the waiting room there suddenly appeared to be a panic next door as nurses and men in white coats were running about and a general hubbub. A little later they came out to tell Don that his wife had quite suddenly died. What had really happened he did not know. They said he could come in and see her, which he did. He was then told he would have to go to the Register Office of Deaths and Marriages. Don was still in shock and wondered whether his wife had been given the best treatment but he did nothing about it as he reasoned it could not bring her back.

He then of course had to ring her mother and give the sad news and then he had to ring Edinburgh to tell Stephen. Frank and Thelma arranged for Stephen to fly down to Heathrow where Don met him. Then there were the funeral arrangements to make and to let other people know and tell them on what day the funeral would be held. Don was worried about what Stephen would wear at the funeral as he did not have a dark suit, however, he was advised that Stephen's blazer would do and that his mother would certainly not have worried what her son wore – he of course had a black tie.

Betty was cremated at the Woking Crematorium and Don wrote a carefully worded epitaph in the book of remembrance. Many people attended the brief service and one of Betty's friends arranged food and drinks back at the house where many people stayed and supported Don for some time.

He told his employers and they were most sympathetic and told him to take time off to recover. He drove Stephen up to Edinburgh and stayed with Thelma and Frank for a few days. On the way back he decided to make a small diversion to show Stephen the last wartime station he was on. However, having driven the twelve or so miles off the main road he was disappointed to find no gate, buildings or blister hangers, instead there were fields of corn with in the middle the remnants of one or two huts. Nothing at all to show that hundreds of American and later British airmen had walked those fields, lived and died there, caught the run to Peterborough, collected their pay, scived, fiddled and worked. It was a journey perhaps one should not have made, but there was something that being near just made him want to see what it was like – but one should not go back.

Back home he learnt that one of Betty's friends had indeed called at the house on the day she had taken the overdose. The friend said she had climbed the spiral staircase at the back of the house as she was concerned when there was no reply at the front door, but she did not try the door to the bedroom which in fact Don discovered was not locked. If only!

He returned to work and a week or two later he had a notice to attend a Coroner's court in Weybridge. Their neighbour from the previous house they had lived in, in Woking, kindly volunteered to come along with him. There were many people in the court and Don had to take the stand and was asked a number of questions by the Coroner, which afterwards the neighbour said he had answered very well. The Coroner finally recorded a verdict of suicide while of unsound mind.

Don was not a church goer but since Betty had been in the Young Wives at a particular church he asked the vicar if there was anything the church wanted and was eventually told they wanted copies of the church's silver candles for display purposes and also they would like to install subdued lighting over the altar. Don paid for these to be done but it was nearly three years afterwards before he was told the work had been carried out. Some time later he went along with Stephen to see what had been done and saw that they had indeed, as requested, dedicated it to the memory of his wife.

Everyone was very sympathetic with Don's situation and as an example for the two following Christmases the next door neighbour kindly invited Stephen and Don to Christmas dinner. In those two years the office had moved from Brixton to Guildford and he had made good progress in the partnership and as the Partnership Administrator was treated all the time the same as partners, having lunch with them every day in the new canteen. His salary had improved and he was getting a good bonus each year.

After moving to Guildford some of those in the partnership decided to take golf lessons at a driving range at Sandown Park and Don joined them, taking Stephen along, where they had some very enjoyable evenings when after golf they returned to the bar for drinks and sandwiches or peanuts. He also started playing badminton once a week and even had one or two games of five-a-side football. He had settled down to his new life but dearly missed his wife.

Chapter Forty-Two

One evening in 1975 two ladies who had been very friendly with Betty paid him a visit with the sole object it seemed of telling him it was time he thought about taking a new wife as it would be good for him and make a better home for Stephen. They made various suggestions and he promised to think about it.

It did make him think; there was a lot of thinking to do and he must not so often waste time looking back. But maybe he should look back just once more and then try to put it to the back of his mind. There was no doubt he had come a long way from when he had first joined the Water Board before the Second World War and he knew he had had a full life, but as the ladies had said he was still relatively young and could have many more years to live. Although he knew it was no good to live in the past, he did get pleasure from remembering the happy times but of course there were sad ones too.

His mind again wandered and he began, as he had done too many times recently, to run through his life. Leaving school in the thirties and starting work in London, yes that was a good time, and he smiled as he remembered the happy times he had had at the Tottenham office, both before and after the war. He thought of old George who went in the Navy and he could see old Smithy coming into the office, resplendent in his RAF officer's uniform, but sadly only a week or so after they had heard he was reported missing, he never returned. He remembered his time as a bouncer/doorkeeper, giving him many happy memories; surely he would never ever ride in a sidecar again, clinging on to a big base drum, whilst all around hell was being let loose. Yes, the Blitz, that was a strange time, guns, bombs and searchlights every night for months on end and yet life carried on. He registered for aircrew, went to dances, cinemas, met girls, played football, went to parties and then the memory of seeing a young lady at an all night party that he was destined to marry. He remembered visiting her, a work evacuee, in the country at Wrest Park, the first time he had seen a country mansion, and then later getting engaged. Yes, there were very happy times, and yet always in the background one knew it could not last, he knew he would soon be called to the 'colours'. He well remembered the operation he had to get into aircrew and, particularly, how he had received the blows in that fair ground fight that had made it necessary. That was something – "I wonder where old Del is now," he mouthed. Finally, being accepted in the RAF and then the long wait until there was room for more recruits to be trained. Lords cricket ground flashed through his mind and some of the many places he was stationed at.

His mind darted through the time in Canada training to be a pilot and the many adventures that accompanied this, particularly in New York, and after eighteen months returning home and the traumatic day of his wedding, his spell in the Middle East, the battle courses at Hereford and later his time as an RAF Accountant Officer. It was not difficult to remember his return to work at the Water Board, when it was soon demonstrated that his wartime service meant nothing. He certainly remembered 'Waste Not Want Not'! Then a few years later came the move to head office when one of his jobs was to work on a building site with John Mowlem.

He remembered the Motor Show and smiled to himself when he thought of how long one was supposed to wait for a new car and how lucky he was to get over this hurdle. Then the tragic death of his sister-in-law followed a year later by the joy of having a son, after almost eleven years of marriage. But happiness did not last as Betty became ill and, like her sister just after the war, she too was sent to a mental hospital. He remembered the visits to the hospital and how every night he took Stephen back from his mother-in-law to look after him until it was time to go to work the next day. How after eighteen years with the Water Board he left for a job in Rugby, which turned out to be disastrous, although he remembered there was one good experience up there as he did successfully teach for a short while in evening school. Then the move back down south to a company with whom for a few years he had much success. As if a dream he recalled the time spent negotiating contracts with Russians, both in Russia and Italy, and his election to the main board of the company and the promise of being the next senior man in the group. Being host to the Russian Ambassador, it seemed unreal and who would believe it now anyway, but it happened. Being the group Chief Executive unfortunately came to nothing due to the American takeover. Then three years later, when, as he put it, 'they had bled my brain', telling him he was no longer wanted, followed, not too long since, by the terrible time of trying to find work, the book he wrote, and after eighteen months when a job had been found being knocked down again by the devastating death of his wife, Betty.

He had to try and forget it all, no not really forget it, but at least try not to waste time consciously remembering. Yes, he had undoubtedly come down from the lofty heights but he was once again gaining respect at work and was getting used to his new position and knew he was doing a worthwhile job and helping an important international partnership of Architects and Engineers who operated all over the world. He was gradually getting back his old confidence and knew his employers were appreciating his skills, particularly in dealing with their bank who had recently told them that but for him dealing professionally with their overdraft situation the partners could have been in real trouble. There had of course been that one partner who tried to speak to him the way the man was apparently used to speaking to any employee, but he only did it once, as Don soon put him in his place and told him in no uncertain terms that he had better not speak to him that way again.

No Don was his own man, now in his fifties; he had learnt a lot and always remembered his dad telling him, "Don't let them get you down, son, remember the bigger they are the harder they fall."

How true!

Don did remarry and has a second son; but that's another story.

END

The following poems, written by Betty, were found among her personal possessions after her death in 1973.

Why Must We Suffer?

How happy little children are as they run about their play!
They have their happy, carefree fun, without a price to pay.
Their cares are very real to them, but how quickly they recover.
They quarrel with a little friend – then lightly find another.
Their tears are shed quite easily, but soon they can forget
The very reason they were shed – and rarely do they fret.
If they've a mother's lasting love they feel so safe and sound,
So sheltered from the world's affairs and troubles all around.
We must be disillusioned though they try to give us warning;
"It's the best time of your life" they say, – the truth in that is
    dawning!

If only we believed it then maybe we could prepare
For what life has in store for us and grow up more aware.
But happiness is worth much more if we can take the pain,
And if there's meaning to this life our suffering's not in vain.

Betty Mary Moggs (1951)

An Escape from the Deep Blue Sea

What is it in this life that does control
These feelings of such blackness and despair?
What can we do to try to overcome them
And bring us that contentment, oh so rare?

We're told so many times to count our blessings,
And when we do they add to quite a few;
And yet they seem to all add up to nothing
When we're overcome by feelings, oh so blue.

There are but few of us who have it in us
To be content with what life has in store;
Too many times we look at other's blessings
And envy them, though we have more.

How can we know what other folk are suffering
When we really know so little how they feel?
They may have everything they need – to others,
And yet have wounds that just don't seem to heal.

Perhaps if we could concentrate on others
We'd find the remedy for our despair;
And find in sharing other people's troubles
That ours are, after all, not much to bear.

Betty Mary Moggs (1953)

To My Husband

Oh how I missed you when you went away,
Each day to me was like eternity.
And yet this I'd not missed for anything –
True value oft springs through anxiety.
How happy am I now that you're returned;
Beloved you are everything to me,
But if time comes when you must go again –
Parted by earth or sky or sea,
Then ever can I wait for you my darling
But let your heart please stay with me.

Betty Mary Moggs (1967)

(Don believes this poem must have been written following his
time in Moscow in 1967.)

My Thanksgiving

Oh GOD! That quantity unknown,
To you I did in desperation turn.
How glad I am that you did not let me down,
But slowly did allow myself to learn
So much more of my true identity.

My humble thanks I offer to you now,
My life to come I must live to the full –
With all those blessings on me you bestowed.
And may that past self not against me pull –
So make my life now most reflect from you.

Betty Mary Moggs (1967)

A Way of Life – For My Son

Give something of yourself to Life
For only when you do,
Will you discover inner light
And joy will come to you.

Life has a strange and eerie way
Of getting back at you,
A hurt you gave to someone
You'll experience anew.

But if you've fellow feeling
And don't let resentment grow
Each time you give a helping hand
Will make your pathway glow.

But don't expect repayment
Your deed must be enough
Just give a little help sometimes
And fear not a rebuff.

Some day you'll be repaid somehow
You may not know quite when,
Yet slowly Time will catch you up
And God will bless you then

Betty Mary Moggs (1969)

The Young In Heart

The young in heart will always see
The beauty of simplicity,
A snowdrop after winter-time,
The shower of a weeping lime
Will cause their step to hesitate
In order to illuminate their day.

The young in heart will always know
The hidden values there below
Someone else not quite as blest
Unable to give of their best,
Who's not discovered that content
Essential for such sentiment and peace.

The young in heart will seek to find
All the blessings here entwined
Which makes our lives upon this earth,
So compound of our grief and mirth
And rich in its intensity,
That all the prize sincerity can win

Betty Mary Moggs (1969)

228

Dear Octopus

It stretches out its tentacles
No matter where you are.
Perhaps you'll try to get away
And travel mighty far.

Dear Octopus, my family,
I love you tenderly,
But were I with you all the time
Methinks you'd stifle me.

With you I never was myself
But what pleased you to be.
How strange it is that now I've changed
You seem to like just 'me'.

Yet you don't really know me
As I myself now know
How near to someone you can be
And not know what's below!

In each and every one of us
There is an inner part,
And there 'tis only he himself
Knows ALL that's in his heart.

Betty Mary Moggs (1969)

Nostalgia

Nostalgia takes me back again
Though I'd say not for me
This rough and tumble every day
And home so late for tea

Yet there's a part in my heart
Where London I hold dear
Just why it is I cannot say
But were I now to hear

The rumble of a rush hour bus
The tramp of all those feet
Wending their way cross London Bridge
Or up from Fenchurch Street

A twinge of longing would I feel
To be there at their side
Passing the Bank and Royal Exchange
And marching down Cheapside

Betty Mary Moggs

(This poem was in rough form and incomplete. Don wrote the last three lines, and hopes Betty would have liked it. It was undated.)